TOP TEN REASONS WHY YOU SHOULD READ THIS BOOK

---

1. You want to leverage the tech brilliance of the youngest workers.
2. You want to learn why younger workers report being lonelier more than other generations.
3. You need a primer on what companies do with data and what privacy laws mean to your business.
4. You want to figure out the right balance of work online and work in real life and what people data has to do with that.
5. You want to build an enduring and smart way to use data to improve employees' work experiences.
6. You want to create an inclusive company culture that connects your employees across locations and generations.
7. You want a sustainable way to provide content and skills to your "learn-it-all" employees.
8. You want to build realness, meaning and belonging in your workplace.
9. You want to find connection in work and life.
10. You want to justify spending more time at the ballpark.

PRAISE FOR DISCONNECTED

"We know that when employees are lonely, they are less engaged, less productive, and more likely to think about quitting their job. Loneliness impacts our employees' health, and also the health of our business. In *Disconnected*, Colleen McFarland examines the importance for business leaders to leverage data and the modern workplace to help our young employees build healthy connections, improving their emotional wellbeing as well as our business performance. "

— **Doug Nemecek, MD, MBA, Chief Medical Officer – Behavioral Health, Cigna**

"Young workers deeply value making a difference in the world, yet they are particularly vulnerable if they feel disconnected from purposeful roles. McFarland identifies that as a result, loneliness, apathy, and a risk for mental health conditions may occur. She also suggests that workplaces can play a role in helping young people find their way in their career development using the very thing that often creates isolation -- digital innovations. *Disconnected* shows leaders ways to use data to help workers and organizations connect, communicate, and enhance operations for greater individual and organizational resilience."

— **Nancy Spangler, PhD, President, Spangler Associates, Workplace mental health consulting**

"People data is key. McFarland does an amazing job of describing how to connect with younger workers to give them a stronger sense of purpose and community at the workplace. *Disconnected* is a must read."

— **Rohin Shahi, author of The Z Factor, How to Lead Gen Z to Workplace Success**

"Our youngest generation is struggling. The statistics are scary. In *Disconnected*, McFarland gives a clear look at how employers can use personalized data and other targeted resources to help improve the employee experience and overall wellbeing of our lonely young workers."

— **Andre Burkholder, MEd, Director of Health Management, Willis Towers Watson**

"Figuring out how to make technology work for us instead of the other way around is one of the most important challenges for this era. As a lifelong business leader and workforce management expert, I can say that the risks for society and the business community in not addressing this issue are real and significant. *Disconnected is* a must read for leaders!"

— **Angela Allen, Interim President/CEO, Human Resources Association of Chicago**

"McFarland has written a book that's really well-timed as businesses struggle to manage people in an era of accelerating change and greater depersonalization. *Disconnected* helps leaders think through how we can and must balance the forces of technology with greater consideration and actioning around teaming, and the human elements that will drive performance of the enterprise for years to come."

— **Donncha Carroll, Partner, Axiom Consulting Partners LLC**

"After two-plus decades of teaching undergraduate students, I've experienced the generational shifts described by McFarland, as well as the powerful impact of changing technology on our lives. *Disconnected* offers intriguing insights about the shifts driven by the new iGen employees, their search for meaningful engagement in their careers, and how organizations may use people data to become more effective."

— **Anne H. Reilly, PhD, Professor of Management, Quinlan School of Business, Loyola University Chicago**

"In *Disconnected*, Colleen McFarland makes an entire generation of young people accessible to the rest of us. With thoughtful insights punctuated by carefully-sourced data, *Disconnected* reads with the pace of a novel and the content of a dissertation. McFarland's book is a must-read for managers who want to energize and maximize the potential of the iGen."

— **Dan Lowman, Senior Vice President & Director, SurveyLab at Grenzebach Glier and Associates**

"With sensitivity and keen insight, author Colleen McFarland offers us a guided tour into the iGen mind and shows us how to assemble and disseminate people data to maximize human impact in the workplace and beyond. *Disconnected* is a valuable tool for any management team and an equally helpful resource for educators, co-workers, parents and anyone else looking to improve their own productivity and social awareness. It is easy to read, informative and an excellent two-way generational bridge."

— **Laura Biskupic, Marketing Director at Winch Financial, and blogger at AnotherSlice.Life**

"The college graduates I am seeing in my management training classes are remarkably different than the millennials. The iGen'ers do not seem to have the same self-confidence and tend to need more reassurance. They seem to need more direction initially but then not need as much follow-up. Their understanding of digital communication is excellent but at times they miss more of the in-person nuances. Read *Disconnected* to get on-point explanations of what this means to managers, as well as concrete suggestions for how to address."
— **Patricia Cook, President of Patricia Cook & Associates, Communications consulting, helping people become "client ready"**

"iGen'ers expect to be trained quickly and be able to use new skills to make immediate contributions in the workplace. As a result, leaders need to recognize the demands of these young workers in order to connect with them and maximize their potential. McFarland's *Disconnected* demonstrates how leaders can use people data to create productive and happy employees."
— **Mary Sue Gurka, Associate Professor, Electrical and Electronic Automated Systems, Joliet Junior College**

"There are four generations in the workplace and each brings important strengths. The challenge employers face is to tap into those strengths and manage generational differences in work styles and expectations around work – life balance. McFarland's *Disconnected* provides employers with a powerful strategy for addressing the need for meaning, data and balance in the iGen."
— **Anita C. Jenke, Executive Director, Career Transitions Center of Chicago**

"iGen is reshaping tech consumption. In *Disconnected*, McFarland demonstrates she understands the honest efforts needed to communicate with iGen, who expect technology to drive communication that is personalized, authentic, transparent and humorous."
— **Sonali Datta, Content Lead, Scalefusion**

"Everybody wants to belong and fit in. From the time we are in junior high, through high school, college and work, we all want to feel a part of something. With social media and technology, one would think it would be easier than ever to fulfill this desire, but actually, that is not the case. Why? In McFarland's book, *Disconnected*, she teaches how people data that already exists on our coworkers can be used to figure out how to better connect with each other at work. When people feel a part of something and valued, productivity goes up, happiness levels go up, turnover goes down and depression goes away. It's a win-win for all!"
— **Cheryl Murphy, Chief Financial Officer, Mercy Home for Boys & Girls**

"In her book *Disconnected*, McFarland explores how we can use the data collected on us to better ourselves in the workplace and outside as well. She reveals that even though we are more connected than ever before, we have lost the personal connection to each other. This tech heavy focus has caused loneliness to rise to epidemic levels, especially among younger generations. In her book, McFarland connects the dots on how we can begin to reverse this and become the best selves we are capable of."
— **Jennifer Garman, Founder & CEO of GratitudeMission.org and author of *Flourish***

"*Disconnected* is a well-researched and timely book. McFarland builds a clear connection between mental health and the digitization of interactivity. Anyone in a leadership position or on track to lead teams should read it."
—**André Buckles, Talent Acquisition Executive**

"*Disconnected* is an insightful journey in how data can be used to help people become their best and the important role leaders in organizations play in deploying data as a tool for personal growth. If you are interested in learning more about the intersection of data, personal growth, and organizational improvement, *Disconnected* is a great resource."
— **Robert Ludke, author of Transformative Markets**

"In a world where technology has enabled constant communication, we're losing our ability to connect. The youngest generations have only known a hyper-connected world. The epidemic of loneliness has real costs — and McFarland connects the dots between available data and its potential for reversing these alarming trends. To quote Peter Drucker, 'What gets measured gets managed,' and *Disconnected* puts the data in the hands of those best-positioned to make the required changes, as well as reap the rewards of doing so. Highly recommended reading for leaders at all levels."
— **Stephanie VanZytveld, Sr. Strategy Consultant, Health Care Service Corporation, and author of *I Am Gold Dust (And You Are Too)***

DISCONNECTED

HOW TO USE PEOPLE DATA TO
DELIVER REALNESS, MEANING,
AND BELONGING AT WORK

COLLEEN MCFARLAND

NEW DEGREE PRESS
COPYRIGHT © 2020 COLLEEN MCFARLAND
All rights reserved.

DISCONNECTED
How to Use People Data to Deliver Realness, Meaning, and Belonging at Work

ISBN	978-1-64137-482-8	*Paperback*
	978-1-64137-484-2	*Kindle Ebook*
	978-1-64137-485-9	*Ebook*

For John, Daniel, and Chris

CONTENTS

PREFACE		XV
INTRODUCTION—THE TIME IS NOW TO USE PEOPLE DATA		1
HOW TO READ THIS BOOK		23

PART ONE		**27**
CHAPTER 1.	PROVIDE EMPLOYEES THEIR PEOPLE DATA	29
CHAPTER 2.	EQUIP YOUR MANAGERS	45
CHAPTER 3.	BETTER THE ONLINE EMPLOYEE EXPERIENCE	67
CHAPTER 4.	DATA PRIVACY AND ETHICS	79

PART TWO		**87**
CHAPTER 5.	TYPES OF PEOPLE DATA	89
CHAPTER 6.	WELLBEING DATA	93
CHAPTER 7.	ENGAGEMENT DATA	103
CHAPTER 8.	PERFORMANCE DATA	121
CHAPTER 9.	PROFESSIONAL DEVELOPMENT DATA	139
CHAPTER 10.	OPERATIONS DATA	149

PART THREE		**157**
CHAPTER 11.	USING PEOPLE DATA	159
CHAPTER 12.	DETECT PROBLEMS. PROMOTE SAFETY	163
CHAPTER 13.	ANSWER QUESTIONS. REAFFIRM	177
CHAPTER 14.	TEST SOLUTIONS. SOLVE PROBLEMS	183
CHAPTER 15.	TARGET OUTREACH	191
CHAPTER 16.	IGNITE GOAL SETTING. MONITOR PROGRESS	205

CONCLUSION	217
EPILOGUE	221
ACKNOWLEDGEMENTS	225
APPENDIX	229

PREFACE

After finalizing the manuscript for this book, my focus shifted and I began working with my publisher on the cover and the interior layout of the book. During this time, the world was hit by COVID-19. As a result, I closed up my desk in downtown Chicago and hauled my computer screens home. I set myself up to work virtually for an undetermined amount of time.

My attention turned to the young adults I interviewed for this book. I reached out to a few of them to check in and see how they were doing and how life had changed for them.

One of them was Molly, a recent college graduate who works for a brewing company in a sales management training program. As we talked about the Coronavirus and how it has changed her work life, she reminded me that since I'd interviewed her, an employee at her company had gunned down five of their coworkers.

"All these horrible weird things keep happening," she said softly.

She continued, "There have been so many mass shootings but I've never been related to one. It was very real, scary and horrible… I could have been there."

During the shooting, Molly kept receiving phone messages from a number she didn't know while she was in a meeting. After the meeting, she checked the messages and learned it was from her company's "Active Shooter System," asking her to verify she was okay and let them know where she was. Molly was with her company's US sales team and leadership, including her CEO, at a conference. Many of them had received the same messages.

Moments later at the conference, the CEO addressed the group of more than five thousand people. He confirmed the tragedy and called off the remaining planned events. He said, "Our family is suffering, and we need to head home."

Molly said, "As horrible a day as it was, I liked how it was handled. I felt proud to be part of the company." She continued, "Also, in a strange way, it was good to hear about it when we were together."

What's also helped is that she and her manager text almost every day. She said he's been pretty laid back, even sending the team memes. She said the work relationship is casual, which is nice because if she has questions, she knows he's going to respond. She doesn't worry about "bothering him."

A few short weeks later, her company began addressing the impacts of the COVID-19 pandemic on their employees too. Molly's job involves going to bars and restaurants, which have been closed or are limited to take-out food. She explained, "Much of my job had revolved around things I can't do anymore."

She explained they have had many calls asking for live feedback on ideas they have for the changing work situation. They'll ask, "Do you think this is something you guys would be interested in doing?" She said it let her know "they really care about their employees and want to be honest."

She told me she was happy to (still) have a job. She told them, "I'll do whatever you guys want." She thought it was good that the leaders looped her and her peers into the conversation. "I think they know that really good ideas can come from the people who are actually doing the job. I think they respect that."

When we spoke, Molly had been sheltered-in-place for one week. She said to me, "This [COVID-19] is very relevant to your book. It's like putting everything to the test that you researched." I knew what she meant. I had been feeling it too.

Disconnected, at its core, is about the need for companies to better connect with their youngest workers by understanding and addressing *their need to feel safe*. I was happy to hear this was happening for Molly with her company.

It's also about how our youngest generation in the workforce now face anxiety and depression at alarming rates, perhaps due to the loneliness that comes from growing up with fewer real-life social interactions than generations before. The COVID-19 crisis requires social distancing for it to be successful. While we all agree this needs to happen, this situation provides us many challenges, one being the risk of emotional distress due to the lack of real-life social interactions. This moment matters for employers. They need to rise to the occasion and get creative with their technology to really connect with employees. Our youngest generation has the advantage of being best able to use technology. Now it's up to the employer to use technologies and other means of communication to truly connect in meaningful ways.

Both during these times of crisis and when it's back to business as usual, I'm hopeful more companies will connect with their employees in a personal way to deliver realness, meaning and belonging at work.

INTRODUCTION—THE TIME IS NOW TO USE PEOPLE DATA

"I don't know how to talk to anyone except my family members."

Two or three times a year, I run an interactive workshop on business networking for a non-profit called Career Transition Center in Chicago. I like CTC's mission, which is to help those who have lost their job for the first time in their career figure out what they want to do next. After each workshop, I leave exhilarated.

Except for the time the workshop included Alicia.[1]

---

[1] Name changed to protect privacy.

I had finished our workshop with twenty participants including Alicia. We had strategized how each of them could build their networks through meeting more people and investing time in getting to know some select people and having an action plan for asking people they know for specific help.

The other participants left the classroom. I was packing up my bag and feeling good about the workshop. It had been interactive—people had shared, people had laughed. Everyone seemed to indicate it was time well spent.

Then Alicia approached me. She was much younger than the other workshop participants, appearing to be in her early twenties. She had her dark hair parted neatly down the middle of her head. She was wearing glasses with frames that made her look serious.[2]

She spoke quietly and as she did, she barely made eye contact with me. She told me "I don't know how to talk to anyone except my family members." She explained that she lived with her parents and her younger brother who was finishing high school. Besides them, she was uncomfortable talking with anyone.

It broke my heart.

I gave her some quick advice about dialoguing more with her family members, then practicing with people when she was out and about—like at Starbucks. As I talked to her she

---

[2] Most of the workshop participants I have had over the years appear to be in their 40s and 50s. Just recently, I have started to get some in their early twenties.

appeared to be listening intently, all the while avoiding my eyes. I could sense something else was going on with Alicia, bigger than needing to work on networking skills.

What I sensed with Alicia continued to nag at me. How hard it must have been for her to listen to all the networking practices discussed that morning. The workshop had been built on the foundation of connecting with people through conversation. I wondered if Alicia's discomfort with conversation contributed to her losing her job, or whether it was something else.

I could not put my finger on what it was with Alicia.

Clearly, she was struggling.

Then I read an article in 2018 by Cigna. They reported that loneliness among Americans has reached "epidemic levels." Cigna's survey of over 20,000 U.S. adults, found that nearly half of survey respondents reported sometimes or always feeling alone or left out. The youngest generation surveyed (ages eighteen to twenty-two) reported feeling lonelier than older ones. More than half of them identified with ten of the eleven feelings associated with loneliness, which included feeling like people around them are not really with them (69 percent), feeling shy (69 percent), and feeling like no one really knows them well (68 percent).[3]

That was it.

---

[3] "New Cigna Study Reveals Loneliness at Epidemic Levels in America."

Alicia was lonely.

Turns out many other young adults like Alicia are struggling too.

I wrote this book because I wanted to learn more about Alicia and other young workers like her who are lonely. And I wanted to know what employers could do to help them.

I found that much of the answer lies in data.

IGEN'ERS COMING TO WORK
The generation entering the workforce now is called "iGen." They follow millennials who were born 1980–1994. They were born between 1995 and 2012.[4]

This new generation is almost everything millennials aren't.[5]

Jean Twenge, a psychologist at San Diego State University is the world's foremost expert on generational differences in American youth. She studies differences in generations including work values, life goals, and speed of development. She analyzes annual survey data collected from American teens. What fascinated me most about her research is how dramatically different this generation is from millennials and what this means to the workplace.[6]

---

4   This generation is also referred to as Generation Z or Gen Z.
5   Twenge, "Meet iGen: The New Generation of Workers That Is Almost Everything Millennials Aren't."
6   Twenge has three iGen daughters, born in 2006, 2009 and 2012.

iGen'ers are more comfortable in their bedrooms than in a car or at a party. Compared to their predecessors, they are physically safer, they're less likely to get into a car accident and they have less of a taste for alcohol. They're incredibly tolerant and have a keen awareness of equality, mental health, and LGBT rights.[7]

They have spent less time socializing in person than any previous generation, because of this some iGen'ers lack social skills. Many are suffering from loneliness. They have grown up more slowly, taking longer to work, drive, and date. They are coming to work with less experience making independent decisions. They will need careful instructions for tasks, and they will need more guidance.

Unlike millennials who demanded praise, iGen'ers want reassurance. They are eager to do a good job, but afraid of making mistakes.

They need managers that are more like therapists, life coaches or parents.[8]

Rohin Shani, author of *The Z Factor* and an iGen'er himself explains that his generation wants to be as prepared as possible for the future. Because of this, they want to be able to learn and develop at work. They are looking for companies

---

7   Twenge. *iGen: Why Today's Super-Connected Kids Are Growing Up Less Rebellious, More Tolerant, Less Happy—And Completely Unprepared For Adulthood (And What This Means For The Rest Of Us).* 312-313
8   Twenge, "Meet iGen: The New Generation of Workers That Is Almost Everything Millennials Aren't."

that will support them and make them "bulletproof for whatever the future holds."[9]

It seems Alicia would benefit from a manager who is part-therapist, part-life coach. I hope at her next job, she gets a manager like this.

IGEN'ERS ON BRINK OF MENTAL HEALTH CRISIS

By looking at the data for people of different generations when they are the same age, Twenge can compare them. She explains that usually the differences between one generation and another gradually present themselves over time. It can take several years for a generational shift to be clear. For example, the differences between baby boomers (1946–1964) and Generation X (1965–1974) were gradually revealed by the annual survey data.

With iGen data, this was different. Beginning in 2010, the annual survey data started showing dramatic differences from millennials. These differences became the defining factors of iGen'ers.

Data from iGen teenagers showed that, compared to millennials at the same age, they were:

- Going out *without their parents* less
- Getting together with their friends informally less
- Feeling left out more
- Feeling lonely more

---

9   Shahi. *The Z Factor: How to Lead Gen Z to Workplace Success*. 158.

Also, more were showing symptoms of depression (*I can't do anything right; my life is not useful, I do not enjoy life*).

Twenge wanted to know why the sudden shift. She learned that what happened was the rise of smartphone usage. In 2012, the number of Americans owning a smartphone crossed 50 percent. "By far the largest change in teens' lives since 2010 has been that more of them got smartphones and they spent more time online and on social media"[10]

Twenge explains that iGen is the first generation to spend their entire adolescence with a smartphone. They have grown up with technology, the Internet, and social media. They don't remember a time before the Internet.[11]

Her data shows that teen depression, smartphone adoption, and "time online" all dramatically increased from 2012 to 2016. She looked into whether iGen'ers who spent a lot of time online were thriving or struggling. She found they were 71 percent more likely to have at least one risk factor for suicide and were twice as likely to be unhappy. In short, they were struggling.

Twenge warns, "It's not an exaggeration to describe iGen as being on the brink of the worst mental-health crisis in decades."[12]

---

10 Ibid.
11 Ibid.
12 Twenge, "Have Smartphones Destroyed A Generation?"

Twenge's warning rang loudly in my ears when I read that the Centers for Disease Control and Prevention recently reported the suicide rate among people ages 10 to 24 years old climbed 56% between 2007 and 2017. CDC also highlighted that in 2017, suicide was the second-leading cause of death among those ages 10 to 24, behind unintentional injuries, such as car crashes or drug overdoses. Several experts believe some of the deaths due to unintentional injuries are related to mental health issues too.[13]

EXPLOITING A VULNERABILITY

A taxi driver who gave me a ride from the Union station in Washington D.C. to the Georgetown neighborhood told me he was from the country of Eritrea. As we talked, I looked up Eritrea on my smartphone. He told me how they warred with neighboring Ethiopia for thirty years until 1991, when they won their freedom. Not having an army or resources, their strategy during the war was to steal Ethiopia's weapons. He told me their battle cry was, "We will kill them with their own weapons."

I thought of this battle cry when I heard Cal Newton speaking on NPR. Newton was being interviewed about his book *Digital Minimalism*. He explained how Facebook had engineered new features (e.g. "likes" and "tagging") to intentionally get people to spend more time on their app. He explained they used knowledge of our brains' vulnerabilities and knowledge of how addiction works to increase the time an individual spends on their app.

---

13 Abbott. "Youth Suicide Rate Increased 56% In Decade, CDC Says."

It worked.

The average time a visitor spends on Facebook went up dramatically since these features were added. Other apps followed suit, adding the same type of features. Today some people are spending ten to twelve hours a day online. It's causing mental health issues for some of them and is linked to the rise in suicides.[14]

In 2017, Sean Parker, the founding president of Facebook acknowledged that addictive features were added to social media. In the video interview with Mike Allen, he says "It's a social-validation feedback loop ... exactly the kind of thing that a hacker like myself would come up with, because you're exploiting a vulnerability in human psychology." "The inventors, creators—it's me, it's Mark [Zuckerberg], it's Kevin Systrom on Instagram, it's all of these people—understood this consciously. *And we did it anyway.*"[15]

When I watched the video, it was not clear to me if Parker felt bad about the harm caused or if he was bragging.

Another technology leader Marc Benioff, Salesforce CEO has been clear about how he feels about the tech-caused harm. He's furious. Benioff has been comparing Facebook to deadly cigarette addiction. He told CNBC "I think for sure technology has addictive qualities that we have to address, and

---

14 Newport, "Avoiding Digital Distraction."
15 Allen. "Sean Parker Unloads On Facebook: "God Only Knows What It's Doing To Our Children's Brains."

that product designers are working to make those products more addictive and we need to rein them back."[16]

I agree with Benioff wholeheartedly that addictive technology and the product designers need to be addressed. I add that this is a leadership issue. These leaders, many who are parents, knew the technology could harm and they allowed it to continue. They used their insider knowledge that this technology was harmful and they protected their own children, as they seductively unleashed it on our children.[17]

As a result, we have a generation harmed.

LACK OF ROOTEDNESS AND CLOSE RELATIONSHIPS
Ben Sasse, who is a historian, may be familiar with the Eritrea battle cry too. He is also someone waving a flag of concern about loneliness. In addition to being a history professor and an author, he is a United States senator from Nebraska. He points to a different impact of technology on society. He cautions that people are not engaging locally and are not rooted in communities.[18]

We are not establishing "a village"—a tight knit group of friends and family that's in our corner. Villages are the groups of people that really know you, understand you,

---

16   Balakrishnan, "Facebook Should Be Regulated Like A Cigarette Company, Says Salesforce CEO."
17   Weller, "Silicon Valley Parents Are Raising Their Kids Tech-Free—And It Should Be A Red Flag."
18   Sasse, *Them: Why We Hate Each Other And How To Heal.* 1-15.

support you, and care about you. A village becomes a foundation from which you can confidently build.[19]

Many of us don't even know our neighbors' names. We have lost our "rootedness." We are not connected by a "place." There is less involvement in civic groups, neighborhood churches, and local youth groups like Little League. Instead people are joining virtual groups with which they engage with online, they are going to mega-churches, and are enrolling their children in activities that are not neighborhood-based.[20]

As a result, many iGen'ers have been socialized differently than previous generations. They grew up knowing many people through activities and have stayed digitally connected to a number of them. Yet many iGen'ers are quite lonely. They don't have many—if any—close friends. These close friends are the type that know what's going on with you and vice versa. You feel safe telling them anything. They understand you and accept you, and you understand and accept them.

iGen'ers are very concerned with safety, including what's called "emotional safety." They want to be protected from offensive comments and emotional upset, just as they want to be protected from physical harm. Some think this is due to their exposure to toxic content and traumatic social situations online. Others think it may be because they didn't have a village and close friends to support them.[21]

---

19 Pinker, "*The Village Effect: Why Face-To-Face Contact Matters.*" 44-72.
20 Sasse, *Them: Why We Hate Each Other And How To Heal.* 1-15.
21 Twenge. "Meet iGen: The New Generation of Workers That Is Almost Everything Millennials Aren't."

What many have missed is the long-term relationships that happen when parents force their children to socialize with the children of people they know. Instead of spending every Saturday at the neighborhood park and Sunday with the relatives or family friends, iGen'ers have spent their weekends participating in organized activities where participants shift from season-to-season and year-to-year.

RESILIENCY

Another difference is the large amount of online socializing that iGen'ers have done without the hint of adult intervention. Bold behavior occurs when there's no fear of an adult "overhearing" a comment. Many have been bullied online and suffered the humiliation that comes with it. Almost all who have spent time online have witnessed bullying and felt ill-equipped to handle it.

For me, growing up in Appleton, Wisconsin in the 1970s and 1980s, one of my main "villages" was my group of cousins, who I saw several times a year at my grandparents' house. We were told to "go play," and that's what we did. While doing it, we learned—how to organize games ourselves, how to fight, how to make-up, how to solve problems, and how to enjoy and appreciate each other. We also knew if anything got out of hand, a parent would sense it and we would have to explain ourselves—this kept us in check. As a result, we learned about relationships and developed resilience.

Relationships can injure. Relationships can also make your heart sing. We become more secure, empathetic and resilient when in healthy relationships, and we can get hurt badly in a relationship that we can't handle. When that happens, often we stop being open to taking the risks that being in an honest relationship requires. Hopefully, this is just for a while, until we've licked our wounds and get up. With experience, we learn the hurt will pass and we will be better again. We become resilient and stay open to others.

Resiliency is a skill that serves you well in the workplace. Because of how iGen'ers developed, at work, they will be risk-adverse and will need to be pushed to step outside of their comfort zone and supported when they do.

At work, they can be challenged to come together with a group of people to tackle a hard problem that seemed impossible, and figure it out. They learn it's OK to be vulnerable and take risks. They can see that a large part of learning is done through making mistakes. With mistakes, they can develop resiliency.

DIGITAL REVOLUTION CONTINUES TO CHANGE WORK
Nowadays, there are less close relationships at work. Fewer of us are going to work in environments where we go to the same place every day and work with the same people, who become part of our "work village." Often, we don't even know the names of the people who sit in the open workspace desks next to us.

Technology has changed work dramatically.

- We don't need to be in the same place to work together. We can work virtually with each other.

- We don't need to verbally dialogue with each other to work together. We can communicate digitally.
- We don't need a company relationship. We can be project-work freelancers or contractors.

Managers will continue to be the force that creates community at work. Just as teachers needed to learn how to educate and bring together tech savvy students, managers will need to learn how to manage tech savvy employees who will often reside in multiple locations.

SKILLS NEEDED FOR REMADE JOBS

Today's digital revolution is similar to the shift to *urbanization* and *industrialization* that happened a hundred years ago. When urbanization happened, people left their close-knit farm communities and moved to cities for jobs. At that time, like now, there was a loneliness crisis. People were afraid. While business was booming, something else was wrong. The influx of people into the cities caused chaos. Sasse explains, "Moms, aunts, dads, and uncles and neighbors were worried America wasn't paying sufficient attention to the social consequences of urbanization." The future was uncertain, and people were scared. The response was prohibition.[22]

Technology, especially automation, continues to impact the workplace. Automation is changing jobs. According to McKinsey analysts, "Fifty percent of activities that people are paid to do in the global economy have the potential to

---

22 Sasse, Them: Why We Hate Each Other And How To Heal 48–49.

be automated by adopting currently demonstrated technology."[23] That means we already have the technology today to automate several parts of jobs.

- OUT of the jobs will be the repetitive activities, replaced by machines.
- IN to the jobs will be activities that require emotional intelligence, communication skills, and creative problem-solving.[24]

Jobs are going to continue to be remade. The uncertainty of what the new jobs will entail exactly causes fear for many employees. What we *do* know is that the new jobs will continue to be more upskilled—the quality, value, and stature of roles will rise. We will need skilled workers to step into these emerging jobs. We will need workers who are both tech savvy and have strong social skills.[25]

The iGen workers are definitely tech savvy and they consume data constantly. This is, in large part, due to the fact that most have spent significant amounts of time with a smartphone in their hand. They don't see technology as a novelty. It's a tool to connect, entertain and aid them in their daily lives. They want to see it used smartly in the workplace but it needs to have a purpose. New communication software used in the workplace like Slack that are used for instant messages is appealing to millennials. But, a majority of iGen'ers want a human factor in the work they do. Rohin Shahi, author of

---

23 McKinsey Global Institute, "Jobs Lost, Jobs Gained: Workforce Transitions in a Time of Automation."
24 Ibid.
25 Sasse, *Them: Why We Hate Each Other And How To Heal.* 55-62.

The Z Factor explains "if I have a question or comment for someone close by in the workplace, I'd much rather walk over to them and talk -beyond stretching my legs, it enables me to have more effective communication than a simple IM or email, and shows that I care about whatever I had to say." A study found that 53% of iGen'ers prefer face-to-face communication over tech-heavy forms of communication like email, video conferencing and, and IM.[26]

EXPECTATIONS OF WORKERS HAVE CHANGED
iGen'ers engage socially online, where it's easy to duck in and out of conversations. They also spend time online as consumers. When iGen'ers visit a site, they are looking for an experience tailored to them. These tailored consumer experiences are possible because of the good work of data engineers and data scientists. They prepare and study large sets of customer data in order to gain insights that result in improved and tailored consumer experiences.

iGen'ers have experienced the benefits of these insights pulled from large sets of data when shopping, reading news, or catching up on social apps and they like it. In fact, sixty-nine percent of consumers now expect this personal digital treatment.[27]

To personalize a digital experience, personal data is needed. Some think young adults don't want their personal data captured and used to market to them. I disagree. I believe they

---

26 Shahi. *The Z Factor: How to Lead Gen Z to Workplace Success*. 41-42, 45.
27 Skeldon, "69% Of Consumers Want An Individualised Customer Experience Yet Only 40% Of Brands Offer One."

are keenly aware of when their data is being captured. In cases where they don't want it to be captured, they tend to know how to avoid it. In other cases, they want the digital data seen and used for their favorite brands to get to know them better, thus provide them a better digital experience.[28]

Matt LoPresti from the premium data company TouchPoints, explained it to me this way, "the more value you provide to individuals when leveraging their data, the more data people will happily share with you."

iGen'ers coming to work will be comfortable working digitally and will be comfortable having their digital data used. They will also be quick to evaluate digital experiences. When their employer uses their data to improve their digital experience, they will notice and be appreciative. When employees' digital experiences are frustrating, it will negatively impact their impression of their employer.

PRIVACY AND SECURITY LAWS
The digital revolution has brought attention to the use of personal information for commerce. Privacy and security laws are in-place now that make it a requirement for some employers to provide some of their employees the personal data they have.[29] Many expect more of these laws soon. There are some that believe employers should be focusing on getting ready to give their employees their data to take with them when *leaving* their company. I say instead, leaders should be focusing

---

28 "Being Watched At Work: Workplace Surveillance Perceptions."
29 Chapter 5 reviews two of the Privacy laws in effect, GDPR and CCPA.

on serving up to their employees their personal data now and do it in a way that impresses and engages them, so they want to *stay* and work on your organization's biggest challenges.

USE PEOPLE DATA TO EVOLVE YOUR ORGANIZATIONS
Organizations are facing a multifaceted challenge.

- The iGen loneliness crisis that's robbed our youngest workers of properly developed social skills is literally causing some of them to die, and others to come to work with wellbeing issues that impact their ability to fully contribute.
- The digital revolution is signaling that winners will be the companies that can develop employees who have strong social skills in order to be able to continuously adapt to emerging remade jobs.
- Workplace anxiousness due to uncertainty around whether companies will retool or discard employees for these remade jobs, is causing some employees to be less engaged.

The answer is to use a resource you already have, **your people data.** People data is all information that pertains to your employees that is generated as part of running your business. It includes data from their annual wellbeing surveys, engagement surveys, performance reviews, professional development plans, and of course all the information generated from operations and business processes—some call this digital exhaust.

Use your people data to make fundamental changes that will dramatically change your workplace and your employees' experience.

Included in this book are three strategies for leaders to consider as they decide what to do first:

1. PROVIDE EMPLOYEES THEIR PEOPLE DATA

First, meet iGen workers where they are: online. Give them their people data in a way that shows them both the way to wellness and how to develop the social skills needed to help your company navigate the digital revolution. Ignite in them the desire to develop the skills needed.

The gravity of the loneliness issue for young adults is known to them. Most iGen'ers personally know people who are suffering from emotional and mental health issues. Companies can—and some already are—blanketing their employees with offers of programs designed to address emotional and mental health concerns through emails, banner ads on the company intranet, and bathroom posters, while well-intentioned, employee mass-outreach is becoming less and less effective. Outreach can instead be personalize when people data is used. We know from the work done with customers' data that if the outreach is smart, well-timed, and customized then participation is more likely.

Inspire young workers to address their individual wellbeing issues by providing them their own people data in a way that demonstrates where action is needed. Also provide it in a way that's mobile, like their smartphone.

2. UPSKILL YOUR MANAGERS

The manager's job needs to be re-made. Their administrative activities are being replaced by automation. Activities being added require a strong foundation of both analytical and social skills. Managers need to have people data to use for managing their employees and themselves. Education is needed for managers to get them savvy with interpreting data and using it to communicate. They also need training to be able to identify employees who are struggling with mental health issues. Additionally, managers need to be equipped to be a coach, therapist, and parental figure for their younger employers, who will be looking for community and connection.

3. BETTER THE ONLINE EMPLOYEE EXPERIENCE

Make online work experiences better. Integrate your people data and use it to gain insights on how to provide meaningful digital experiences, that both get work done and connect employee communities.

You simply need to have better digital experiences for employees. Single sign-on is not enough. Younger workers expect their digital experience at work to be smart—which is what they experience as consumers.

When digital experiences at work are not smart, these sub-par experiences taint the impression that an employee has about their organization. iGen'ers want to work for a company of which they are proud.

While people data is used for various management reports, not many organizations are integrating it and using it to gain insights.

You are not harvesting this rich resource the way many of you do with your consumer data. Consumers' digital experiences have been improved. It's time now to use your people data to improve your employees' digital experiences, and their overall experience working at your company.

Leaders,

The time to use people data is now. Should you take no action, the iGen'ers who saw their colleges as behind the times and irrelevant in our fast-paced world of constantly changing technology, will be just as quick to pass judgement on your organization.[30]

Additionally, these data-savvy transparency-seeking younger workers will want to see their people data. Privacy laws are going to make it possible for even more employees to get their personal data from their employers. Despite their need for security, iGen'ers will take their data and the tech-skills they developed under your watch and go somewhere else, unless you make them want to stay.

You have an opportunity to go beyond adhering to the letter of the privacy laws and evolve your organization to a place that provides connection.

---

30   "iGen Quotes By Jean M. Twenge."

iGen'ers will pick-up new technology and adapt to workplace changes easily. Know that they want to work and add value quickly, so be ready to give them challenging assignments. Pair the assignments with direction to work on developing essential social skills. When you do, they will find connection in the workplace community you have welcomed them to join.

Using your people data to connect your people will signal to them that you are a company for future—a company that delivers realness, meaning, and belonging at work.

HOW TO READ THIS BOOK

There is a lot to know about People Data.

Treat the table of contents of this book like a drop-down menu. Scan for what you want to learn more about and go directly there.

IDENTIFY WHAT YOU WANT OUT OF THIS BOOK
Having a clear outcome is a powerful yet often overlooked tactic when reading a non-fiction book.

This book has numerous stories that will help you understand and remember how people data can be used for good, and why the time is now to start leveraging it.

Consider a few questions you want this book to answer for you. Then go look for the answers. Treat each chapter as an independent study guide on a specific topic.

Do not let the pressure of needing to finish this book prevent you from starting. Even though some chapters are connected, most of them stand on their own. Just read the ones that grab your attention and, more importantly, prompt you to take action as a leader.

No one chapter can turn you into a data scientist or data engineer, but each chapter has the power to give you acumen to push for doing more in your organization.

ONLY USE THE STRUCTURE AS A GUIDE
The structure of the book is made up of three main sections, with subgroups under each section. This structure is put in place to help you better understand the book's contents. Many chapters are interconnected and can fall into different sections and groups. Do not let the structure limit you. Jump into any chapters that interest you.

Chapters 1–4 explain why companies should use their people data.

Chapters 5–10 give an overview of the most typical types of people data.

Chapters 11–16 provide examples of how people data has been used beyond the activities that created it.

TAKE ACTION

Knowledge is not power. Knowledge is only potential power. Nothing will happen unless you take action.

Reflect on what you as a leader can do to leverage the asset of your people data. How can you help your company achieve its mission by using people data? How can you drive the change needed in your culture to welcome and engage younger workers by using people data? Then set a goal and get to work.

PART ONE

CHAPTER 1
PROVIDE EMPLOYEES THEIR PEOPLE DATA

Richard keeps his feet firmly planted as his train car moves steadily over the bridge. He looks east out the window at the river. His eyes strain to see if they can spot Lake Michigan. The grip of his left hand is loose on the strap attached to the ceiling. His right hand is gripped tight around his iPhone.

The latest Barstool podcast is playing in his AirPods. His smartphone vibrates. He turns his gaze to his phone and sees a news alert, it's another deadly mass shooting: five people killed at a bank in Florida. With his free hand he scrolls his Instagram. He smiles at a jab given to his friend Charlie by his brother Joe. He checks his bank app to see if his direct deposit has shown up yet.

The train slows to a crawl and the riders begin jostling toward the door. The recorded announcement blares: "Washington is next. The doors open on the right. Please keep your belongings off the seat next to you so others may sit down."

The train stops. "This is Washington." The doors open. Richard makes his way slowly to the door and exits along with most of the others on the train car, careful to make no eye contact with any of them.

Richard is afraid of failure. Yet, if you met him when he's wearing his tailored suit and easy smile, you would not see this. He's polished, likable, and carries himself with an air of confidence as he walks the streets of the Chicago Loop. However, since he started his dream job last month, at a prestigious financial institution, he has been filled with self-doubt.

This day he gets his Starbucks coffee then settles into his desk. He opens an email from his Human Resources partner. It states that his Integrated Wellbeing information has been updated and is available through his People Data Dashboard. The email states that the Integrated Wellbeing information is collected by a third party and is confidential. It has a link. Richard clicks the link and is taken to a screen full of colorful charts, graphs and tables titled "Richard's People Data." As he scans the page, he can tell the information is about him.

His eyes bounce around as he takes in the page. He sees the details from his resumé and what looks like the results of a test he took while interviewing. His eyes stop at a chart with four quadrants titled "Your Wellbeing Indicator." He scrolls over the title and reads, "Your Wellbeing Indicator measures your current wellbeing in physical, emotional, social, and financial terms; it identifies areas of strength and high performance, and helps you pinpoint where you need to focus to build your wellbeing, productivity, and overall business performance and track progress over time. These are the results of your most recent Health Assessment Survey." Richard recalls taking a survey when he selected his health benefits the day he started.

The quadrant titled "social wellbeing" is bright red. He sees in the chart's key that the "red" signifies this score is low and action is recommended. He sees a bolded link that reads "action options" underneath the wellbeing chart. He clicks this link. Then a bright yellow page opens. Its title is "Social Wellbeing."

Richard scans the section and comes to understand that social wellbeing is about being connected to others and applies both to the workplace and your personal life. It requires skills related to having stronger relationships like knowing how to support and collaborate with others, being able to successfully resolve conflicts, and adapt to change.

On the screen he sees suggested videos, articles, and support services related to social wellbeing. He decides to look this over when he gets home. He closes the screen and goes back to his inbox.

Later that evening, after polishing off his dinner, he opens his laptop and navigates to back to his People Data Dashboard and the bright yellow "action options" section. He watches some videos and reads some articles that explain that action is needed. Those with low social wellbeing scores—like his—will find themselves with declining physical wellbeing and emotional wellbeing if no action is taken. He comes to understand that wellbeing facets are related to one another. Richard sees he needs to address his low "social wellbeing" score. He reviews the support options and determines that of the support services offered he likes the wellbeing coach option most. They can meet over the phone, or on a web app like Skype.

He also likes that wellbeing coaches usually refrain from giving direct advice or solving their client's problems—rather, they ask questions and guide. Plus, he's wondering if the coach will help him to understand his self-doubt problem too.

He requests the wellbeing coaching services and the next day receives an instant message from Terry, the coach. They make plans to meet over Skype the following week, before Richard heads off to work.

After three months of coaching support, Richard takes a follow-up Health Assessment. He can tell as he answers the questions that he has made progress. After the last question, he presses submit. He's then directed to the chart that compares the survey he just completed to the one he took earlier. He can see the progress clearly. The social wellbeing score is no longer red. It's now yellow, which means he still has work to do but is progressing. He closes the report and makes a mental note to look it over that night.

PROVIDE EACH EMPLOYEE AN INDIVIDUALIZED PEOPLE DATA DASHBOARD

Having data to show progress on wellbeing will motivate your employees to work at being well—especially if you customize the support offerings. One way to provide the wellbeing data is through an individualized people data dashboard, like the one just described.

Wellbeing data is one type of people data. People data is also known as employee data. It's defined as datasets describing people in organizations. It is the information you have available on your various pools of people, collected from any one of your systems such as Human Resources Information System.

Included in an employee's dashboard could be all the people data you have on that individual. Including the sets of data that will be addressed in this book:

- Wellbeing: Annual health assessment data.
- Performance: Current and past performance reviews.
- Professional Development: Current and past development plans.
- Engagement: Company engagement survey data and individual data and teams data.
- Operations: Activity from operation and business processes. For example, data from video meetings, phone calls, security badges, MS Office 365

You want each data type to summarize the information in a way that entices the employee to engage with it. You want the data to encourage them to set maintenance or improvement goals, and to monitor those goals.

The youngest workers want to see how their journey is tied to their company's journey. They need to know they are a pivotal part of that journey. In the dashboard include information about your company's ambition for the future. Say where you want the company to be in five years. Explain that as the company grows, the employee can grow too. [31]

I discussed the People Dashboard concept with Dr. James J. Mazza. He is a Professor in the College of Education at the University of Washington. Specifically, he is an expert in the field of adolescent mental health. Dr. Mazza's research focuses particularly on adolescent internalizing disorders such as depression, anxiety, posttraumatic stress disorder, exposure to violence, and—especially—suicidal behavior.

Teens and college students are learning skills for emotional problem-solving because of the good work of Dr. Mazza and his colleagues. One of the tools used in his course is a daily "diary card" that the student uses to track progress.

Dr. Mazza has seen in his research what I see in the workplace: that using data to track behavior changes works.

"There's credence to the idea that when people track their own behaviors, whether it's financial, whether it's mood, whether it's calories, that it does impact their future behaviors," Mazza says. "I think it is enough to suggest that when

---

[31] Shahi. *The Z Factor: How to Lead Gen Z to Workplace Success.* 35.

people have a daily tracking of their behaviors, that it gives them information to help them try to reach the goals that they've established for themselves."

We talked about the social element of some tracking apps like Fitbit, the activity tracker that tracks the number of steps walked. I brought up Venmo, an app where you can transfer funds to others. I find it fascinating that people share with all their contacts the details of who they have transferred money to and the reason why. Sometimes the reasons are meant to get a laugh. This tells me the users are having fun with the data. Dr. Mazza explained to me the Venmo behavior, to him, is about demonstrating attachment.

"With our societal changes, young adults are not having as many opportunities to socialize in-person because they're busy with their screens doing independent, individual things," he says. He explains that sharing who you are sending money to provides you an opportunity to show your relationship to the person. Plus, if you share that you have sent money to a charity, it provides an opportunity for others to see this and appreciate that charity is doing something you care about. Venmo is giving you a way to share something about yourself with others.

HAVE SOCIAL ELEMENTS WITHIN THE DASHBOARD
Include a way to share goals and progress toward goals with others. Young adults share personal information through their social apps. Just as they use those apps to demonstrate attachment, they will welcome the opportunity to digitally

do the same at work. The individualized people data dashboard can give them a place to do this.

Providing people data to your employees in an engaging way will inspire them to set goals and monitor their results. Your youngest workers will respond, and you will see better overall employee wellbeing, engagement, and performance.

INCLUDE VISIBLE MARKERS IN DASHBOARD
A large financial services company experienced how eager employees are for learning. An executive at the company told me she rolled out LinkedIn Learning to 5,500 of her company's employees. Sixty percent of them tried it out and thirty percent became incredibly active on the optional tool.

"Look, we're doing barely any commercials, nothing really. And still, in the last year, our average is 45,000 videos a quarter being watched…I think this points to how hungry our associates are (for learning)," the leader explained.

The company also implemented Degreed, a service that both offers learning content and shows employees what they have been learning. The executive explained that Degreed provides visible markers that demonstrate to the employee what they are learning and reinforces continued learning.

Showing an employee what they have been learning, and could learn alongside their other people data will give them insights that they can't see when the information isn't connected.

WELLBEING PROGRAM AND RETURN ON INVESTMENT CONSIDERATIONS

Today we are spending more time online than on any other activity including sleeping—up to eleven hours a day. Research shows that this is having an impact on our wellbeing.[32]

Dr. Nancy Spangler works with leaders to develop strategies for prevention, early detection, and management of chronic and costly health conditions. A large portion of Dr. Spangler's career has been devoted to workplace population health management, and she currently focuses on the contributions of mental wellbeing and resilience to workplace performance.

She explained to me that many companies are now seeing that wellbeing is more than just physical health. Negative emotional, social, and financial conditions can also hurt employees' ability to focus on work, interact effectively with others, and maintain energy required for creativity and goal completion.

When considering how to distribute funds for wellbeing programs across the different wellness areas of physical, psychological, social and financial wellbeing, leaders should reference Dr. Julianne Holt-Lunstad's research. She is a professor of Psychology and Neuroscience at Brigham Young University

---

[32] Pinker. "Transcript Of "The Secret To Living Longer May Be Your Social Life.""

Holt-Lunstad set out to answer the universal questions asked by many: "When am I going to die?" and "How can I put that day off?" She conducted a series of interviews and studies of tens of thousands of middle-aged people. She looked at every aspect of their lifestyle: diet, exercise, marital status, doctor visits, smoking, and drinking habits. She recorded it and put it away.

After seven years, she pulled it out. Then she and her colleagues determined which of those people she'd interviewed were still alive, studied the data and came to understand what reduced their chances of dying the most. She called her findings "The Greatest Contributors to Staying Alive."

They were:

- Social Integrations
- Close Relationships
- Quit Smoking
- Quit Boozing
- Flu Vaccine
- Cardiac Rehab
- Exercise
- Lean vs. Overweight
- Hypertension Rx
- Clean Air

I asked Dr. Spangler to look at the "Staying Alive" list and let me know whether or not companies were currently offering programs related to each them. She let me know that companies are offering programs that help support employee wellbeing in a variety of ways (educational programs, opportunities for healthy eating, exercise, quiet break areas for stress recovery, etc.).

She added, "The employers who also support employees' ability to make a difference at work (i.e. to bring their best gifts and talents to their jobs, connect effectively and respectfully with others who share similar values and goals, and to make a difference together in tangible ways), they are supporting true wellbeing at work."

Holt-Lunstad's research says wellbeing programs that encourage employees to connect are also doing more to help them "stay alive." See figure 1.[33]

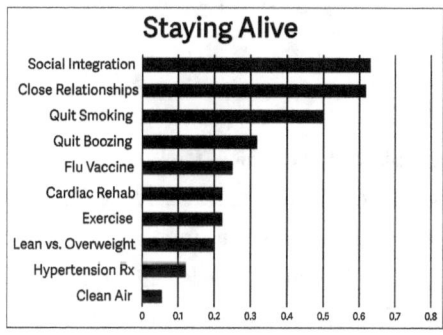

Figure 1: Staying Alive[34] [35]

---

33 Ibid.
34 Ibid.
35 Comparison of odds (lnOR) of decreased mortality across several conditions associated with mortality. Effect size of zero indicates no effect. The effect sizes were estimated from meta analyses.Julianne Holt-Lunstad, Timothy B. Smith, and J. Bradley Layton. 2010. "Social Relationships And Mortality Risk: A Meta-Analytic Review". *Plos Medicine* 7 (7): e1000316. doi:10.1371/journal.pmed.1000316.

The top contributing "Staying Alive" factors are Social Integrations and Close Relationships.

SOCIAL INTEGRATION
This means how much you interact with people as you move through your day. How many people do you talk to? This means both your weak and your strong bonds, so not just the people you're really close to and who mean a lot to you. For example, do you talk to the guy who makes you your coffee every day? Do you talk to the train conductor? Do you talk to the woman who walks by your house every day with her dog? Do you attend a trivia night, play rat hockey, participate in a golf league, or have a book club? Do you play on a softball team?[36]

ADDRESSING SOCIAL INTEGRATION
Social integration means interacting by talking to people in-person. Interacting online doesn't count. In her book, *The Village Effect: How Face-to-Face Contact Can Make Us Healthier and Happier,* Susan Pinker explains how in-person interactions give you a benefit you don't get from digital contact.

"Face-to-face contact releases a whole cascade of neurotransmitters, and like a vaccine, they protect you now in the present and well into the future," Pinker says.

---

36 Pinker. "Transcript of 'The Secret To Living Longer May Be Your Social Life.'"

When you make eye contact with somebody, shake hands or give somebody a fist bump, it is enough to release oxytocin. Doing this increases your level of trust and lowers stress levels. Dopamine is generated, which gives us a little high and kills pain. It's like a naturally produced morphine.[37]

CLOSE RELATIONSHIPS

These are the people that you can call on for a loan if you need money suddenly, who will call the doctor if you're not feeling well, or who will sit with you if you're in despair during an existential crisis. Those people, if you have them, are a strong predictor of how long you'll live. Research says you need at least three people like this in your life.[38]

ADDRESSING CLOSE RELATIONSHIPS

In my business networking workshop, "How Wrigley Field Made Me a Better Networker," we talk about how we all have people in our lives who make up our network. I teach about the need to make networking a way of life in order to create a vibrant village of people who encourage us. Turns out, spending time on developing relationships isn't just important for business networking—it's also important for your wellbeing. Encourage your employees to consider embracing some networking practices. Offer them the practices from my workshop, *What Wrigley Field Taught Me About Networking*. See figure 2.

---

37 Ibid.
38 Ibid.

Which of these Networking Practices Do You Do?

A=Always, S=Sometimes, N=Never

Meeting More People	A	S	N
Introduce yourself to someone you don't know at an event/party.	☐	☐	☐
Ask people you meet about their work/profession.	☐	☐	☐
Engage with people on social media to meet them (i.e. LinkedIn, Twitter).	☐	☐	☐
Attend larger (more than 10 people) networking events put on by others.	☐	☐	☐
Participate in formal organizations (i.e. professional, religious, hobby/special interest, political, charitable) or work on passion projects/side gigs.	☐	☐	☐

Getting to Know More People	A	S	N
Exchange "elevator speeches" and stories.	☐	☐	☐
Consciously use "active listening" techniques in conversations.	☐	☐	☐
Join or lead a formal organization's group such as a committee (professional, religious, hobby/special interest, political, charitable).	☐	☐	☐
Invite someone to network "over coffee" – less than 30 minutes.	☐	☐	☐
Invite someone to lunch, drinks or dinner – 1 hour plus.	☐	☐	☐
Engage digitally with someone by exchanging thoughts and ideas.	☐	☐	☐

Connecting People	A	S	N
Introduce a small group (2-3 others) to each other at event hosted by you.	☐	☐	☐
Host a large (4 or more) event for people to meet or re-connect with others.	☐	☐	☐
Spend time considering who you should connect and why.	☐	☐	☐
Introduce people to each other at events/meetings.	☐	☐	☐
Introduce people to each other over email – "5-minute favor."	☐	☐	☐

Asking for Help	A	S	N
Set a goal and strategy for achieving it that includes leveraging your network.	☐	☐	☐
Clearly articulate what you need help with.	☐	☐	☐
Ask for help from someone you "know and are current with."	☐	☐	☐
Reach out to someone "you know and are not current with" to ask for help.	☐	☐	☐
Ask someone you don't know for help.	☐	☐	☐

Adapted from "What Wrigley Field Taught Me About Networking."

Figure 2: What Wrigley Field Taught Me About Networking

Leaders,

Data is needed to ignite your data-driven employees to take action. Provide employees their people data along with resources to ignite their passion to embrace healthy lifestyle choices as a way of life, along with meeting their performance goals and progressing on professional development.

iGen'ers are practical, yet cautious. Show them you understand them by satisfying their need for good, current data that tells them where they stand relative to their goals and how they are progressing. When you do, they will work hard, and their potential is without limit.[39]

---

39 Twenge. *Meet iGen: The New Generation Of Workers That Is Almost Everything Millennials Aren't.*

CHAPTER 2

EQUIP YOUR MANAGERS

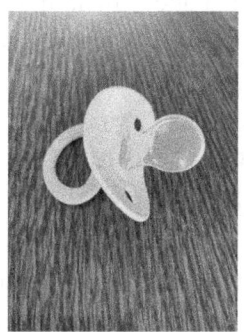

In 2001, when I was first back to work after my son Chris was born, I distinctly remember being in a difficult meeting with some co-workers. We were intensely discussing a critical topic. I was doing my best to listen to their concerns taking notes while I did so. Then my pen stopped working. I tried to reach into my purse discretely to pull out another pen, when my hand bumped into one of my son's pacifiers. Without giving it too much thought, I put the pacifier on the conference room table and looked around at my colleagues with a smirk on my face.

The conversation stopped.

Then we all had a good laugh. They asked me about my newborn and his big brother Daniel. It brought a moment of much-needed levity to the meeting. Then we got back to work.

Around ten years later, I remember delivering a two-hour training session to a team. I had asked the group to stay engaged, which meant no side conversations, no phone calls, no text messages. After about an hour, I could tell the group needed a break. They were fidgeting. So, I called a break. As I did, one-by-one each person grabbed their smartphone and quietly looked at it, as they tapped and scrolled through messages. They didn't engage with each other. They didn't even get up out of their chairs.

Reflecting on it later, it made me think of the pacifier incident. The act of looking at the smartphone seemed to calm the training participants down. It was what they needed to relax. They needed it the way the pacifier group a decade earlier needed to laugh together.

What I've learned is we humans are a deeply, profoundly social species. In fact, our brains grew to our current size, scientists say, in order to process our complex social interactions. We *need* connection to be well. Our smartphones have become an extension to our world. They connect us, reassure us—some might even venture to say they comfort us the same way a pacifier comforts an infant.[40]

---

40   Pinker. *The Village Effect: Why Face-To-Face Contact Matters.* 209-211

YOU WILL FIND IGEN ONLINE

To recap: this workforce's youngest workers are called iGen. Generational researcher Jean Twenge defines them as anyone born between 1995-2012. The oldest of them finished college in 2017 and consequently entered the workforce. iGen has grown up with technology, the Internet, and social media. They don't remember a time before the Internet.[41]

When iGen'ers were in their pre-teen and teen years they spent a lot of time online. In fact, they spent more time online than they did sleeping. They checked their phones an average of eighty times a day. They have been interacting on social media with each other for years. Most go online to seek answers, rather than asking someone in their normal, everyday life.

Online life has become so intertwined with our offline lives, that the abbreviated phase "IRL" is being used as shorthand for "in real life" to distinguish which experience someone is referring too. IRL describes when someone is indicating they are talking about normal, everyday life and not talking about digital lives, like something that happens in games, social media, or television.

Spending less time IRL has meant less in-person social interaction with the people and the close relationships that come from time together in-person.

---

41   Twenge. "Meet iGen: The New Generation Of Workers That Is Almost Everything Millennials Aren't."

Research is showing iGen has more mental health issues than generations before them at the same age. Twenge believes fewer in-person interactions and the rise of smartphones are the reason for the increase in mental health issues with iGen. Many experts acknowledge there is a crisis of loneliness and at its core is the lack of interactions IRL.[42]

IGEN SKILLS NEEDED

We are going through a digital revolution. Technology continues to rapidly change how we work. The youngest workers are bringing tech-savvy skills needed to handle this revolution and its ever-changing landscape. They embrace technology: Eighty-six percent of them believe that new technologies create jobs. Young adults will master the technical part of their jobs and be ready for the next challenge. Both to retain iGen workers and ready them for jobs of the future, managers need to call to their attention the importance of them working on the relationship part of the job and associated social-emotional skills.

Not only will these skills be lacking—due to how iGen has developed—these very skills are the ones you will *need* often from your new workers. As repetitive activities are replaced by machines, jobs are going to be remade to include activities that require these skills. The good news is that, in general, iGen workers *want* to develop new skills. With prompting and resources, they will address their skills gaps.

---

42 Twenge, *iGen: Why Today's Super-Connected Kids Are Growing Up Less Rebellious, More Tolerant, Less Happy--And Completely Unprepared For Adulthood*, 101-102

These young adults are on their way to work, so prepare your managers. [43, 44]

Managers of iGen Checklist

☐ Provide managers people data in a tool
☐ Show your managers how they are performing frequently
☐ Provide access to company statistics and policy information so that managers may demonstrate integrity, honesty, and transparency
☐ Push employees to develop "in real life" skills
☐ Have programs in place to help employees struggling with mental health issues
☐ Promote camaraderie and safety on-line and IRL with employees

1) PROVIDE MANAGERS PEOPLE DATA IN A TOOL

"We want to create a manager dashboard," says Katie Coleman, human resources executive at TransUnion. She explained to

---

43 Social-emotional (SE) skills include the knowledge, attitudes, and skills necessary for a person to recognize and control their emotions and behaviors; establish and maintain positive relationships; make responsible decisions and solve challenging situations; and set and achieve positive goals. Sometimes labeled as twenty-first century skills, soft skills, non-cognitive skills, or character attributes, SE skills have been shown to be malleable and linked to academic, career, and life success. Based on this evidence, promoting these skills in young people has become a priority for both schools and afterschool settings. "Social-Emotional Skills." Home, Toolkit, *Nationalmentoringresourcecenter.Org*. Accessed on January 24, 2020.

44 Batbington-Ashaye, "What Do Young People Care About? We Asked 26,000 of Them."

me that the global information and insights company has been, "focusing on creating awesome managers."

The dashboard is the number one pillar of their strategy. Coleman envisions the dashboard having data that can "pinpoint where a manager might be lagging." While they are still tossing out ideas of what it would be and how they could measure being an awesome manager, she imagines it will include basic items like performance, engagement, diversity and inclusion metrics, and hiring data. But it would also have a way to measure team member development.

Coleman is quick to say that part of providing data to managers is educating them on how to make sense of the data and how to incorporate the data into conversations they have with employees.

Leveraging people data for use by managers, the way TransUnion is planning to do, makes sense. Give your managers a better tool for accessing and understanding the people data you have.

2) SHOW YOUR MANAGERS HOW THEY ARE PERFORMING FREQUENTLY

A management consultant, Royal Rarick, told me the story of a tech company with around 1,200 employees that was working to keep their strong "culture of openness." They decided to measure the openness component of culture quarterly with an employee survey, with each respondents' answers being attributed to their name. When they communicated this decision to employees, management encouraged them to participate in an open dialogue process of honest self-examination for the organization. They explained that managers would promptly receive their team's results, the results of others, and would open any follow-up dialogue with employees as needed.

The survey used an agreement scale such as Agree/Tend to Agree/Tend to Disagree/Disagree. It had statements like, "My manager communicates consistently to me about my performance," and, "I consistently have coaching sessions with my manager." Managers received not only their results but also the results of their peers. Plus, they were able to look at past survey data easily from the tool's dashboard. The surveying process sent the message, "We are serious about these behaviors. They matter."

Putting engagement data into the hands of the employee is also possible. The employee could see what part of their experience at work is not working for them—be it their current role, manager, or work-life balance. They could see the engagement results of others in their organization and compare. Suggested action plans could be given that correspond to their results, where an employee or manager could select an action to take, then a check-in prompt could be sent at a later time to check completion and effect.

Providing frequent engagement data to managers, like this tech company did, helps a manager self-monitor their behavior.

3) PROVIDE ACCESS TO COMPANY STATISTICS AND POLICY INFORMATION SO THAT MANAGERS MAY DEMONSTRATE INTEGRITY, HONESTY AND TRANSPARENCY

Young adults consume data constantly. They rarely take information at face-value. They are suspicious and dig into online content to better understand what's real. According to an annual poll by the World Economic Forum's Global Shapers Community, most young adults see themselves as global citizens. They are plugged into current events and have concerns, e.g. climate change, destruction of nature, threat of war, and religious conflict. They are looking for leaders with integrity, honesty, and transparency.[45]

Employees will bring public data to work and ask about it. Managers need to be ready for these discussions. Equip your managers with company data, including people data. Provide it in a way that managers can easily consume and reference. Educate them on how to work with the data, how to communicate data, and use data to communicate.

Crucially, establish policies around ethical use of data. Put controls in place to ensure employees are adhering to policies. Identify and remove unethical leaders and be transparent when you do. By having current information in the hands of managers who can confidently speak to it, managers can be leaders who are transparent, honest, and operate with integrity.

---

[45] Babington-Ashaye. "What Do Young People Care About?"

4) PUSH EMPLOYEES TO DEVELOP IN REAL LIFE (IRL) SKILLS

My friend Gina told me her eighteen-year-old daughter Julia was reserved and struggled with anxiety. She didn't talk much at all, especially to people she didn't know.[46]

When Gina was thinking about Julia heading to college for her freshman year, she thought that work experience would help Julia with her confidence. Gina was able to secure Julia an internship at her agency in downtown Chicago. Because they lived in the suburbs, Gina also thought the experience of coming to work downtown would be an adventure for Julia.

Julia was assigned to work in the digital marketing group, and she was excited. Like many young adults she was very comfortable with anything digital. Her manager was a middle-aged man named Tom.

On Julia's first day, Tom gave Julia an assignment to look up all the retail businesses within two miles of their location. Julia quickly finished this task. She reviewed the list with Tom. He was complimentary of how quickly she had compiled the list. Julia felt good.

Then, Tom looked at Julia and told her he wanted her to go to some of these locations (there were close to a hundred on the list) and ask them if they would be willing to put a flier up at their location advertising an event the agency was having. They selected some and mapped out her walking path.

---

46 Names changed to protect privacy.

As Julia headed out her stomach quickly turned—she felt ill. She was afraid because she didn't know her way around the city. Also she was severely anxious about talking to people and asking them to do something. She was full of dread. She texted her mother asking for help.

As Julia started out on her journey, she kept her mother on the phone. Her mother provided directions and moral support the whole way. Julia would hang up with her mother just before entering an establishment, then call back after the task. To Julia's (and her mother's) surprise, Julia got twelve approvals in a row! Gina told Julia how proud she was of her and what a great record she had so far—twelve out of twelve!

MANAGER IN THE KNOW
The next day, Gina asked her co-worker and Julia's manager Tom, "Did you know asking Julia to get flyers hung in the stores would be really hard for her?"

Tom said he did know that. That was a big part of the reason why he asked her to do it and do it on her first day. Tom shared with Gina that when he was younger, he had had many of the same fears and anxieties that Julia has. He told Gina his first manager had him do a similar task that was uncomfortable for him.

Looking back, he appreciated how getting the push from his manager had helped him. He wanted to push Julia in the same way, and also let her know her job was more than just working on a computer.

A manager like Tom knows that you need social skills no matter what your job is. He could have easily kept Julia behind the computer all summer. Instead he pushed her to grow—and grow on her first day no less!

BASELINE SKILLS

As a manager, it's easy to divide labor among your team members by assigning them duties they are comfortable with, and in some cases this approach makes sense.

For example, a manager could have some team members handle all the analysis and have others do all the in-person outreach. *StrengthFinder 2.0* talks about how each of us should know our strengths, and when it comes to development it claims that it's actually a better strategy to spend time developing your strengths versus working on your weaknesses.[47]

While I agree with this strategy overall, I think everyone needs to have a baseline of skills in order to be secure in their ability perform well at work. A job market research firm analyzed twenty-five million online job postings from more than 40,000 sources. They found employers want baseline skills such as communication, writing, and organization, plus they expected those entering office-based jobs to be skilled in the Microsoft Office suite.[48]

---

47 The Clifton StrengthsFinder is an online assessment that helps individuals identify, understand and maximize their strengths. It has an accompanying book, StrengthsFinder 2.0.
48 Rapacon, "The Skills Employers Are Looking For."

In today's business world, it's important to be both proficient at working with digital information *and* with people face-to-face. You need to be able to understand the numbers and also be able to interpret them. You need to be able to read through the data, then have a conversation about it. In business you also need to be able organize your point of view using data and deliver it verbally and visually in a presentation. You need to be comfortable and proficient engaging in-person at work.

EMPLOYEE RESOURCE GROUPS[49]

A leader told me she had been in a role that was isolating. Because of the nature of that job, she wasn't interacting with many other employees. She felt the most disconnected she had ever felt since she joined her company.

She decided to join an employee resource group sponsored by her company. Employee resource groups (ERGs) are groups of employees who join together in their workplace that have common interests, backgrounds, or demographics. Being involved with the ERG gave the leader an opportunity to see people, who she didn't typically work with in a different way. She found herself making the time to do work to support the em-

---

49 Many companies have mature ERGs. A good example is Dell Technologies. They have thirteen groups including Asians in Action, Caregivers, Black Networking Alliance, Latino Connection, Women in Action, Pride and Veteran and Supporters. "Award Winning Employee Resource Groups." About Dell, Diversity & Inclusion, Employee Resource Groups. *Dell*.com. Accessed February 1, 2020.

ployee resource group despite how busy she was. It was an empowering experience for her.

The experience caused her to reflect on the need for what she calls "helping people with the first step." The leader explained that she worries a lot about introverts, which she describes herself as. She said that "sometimes the way we prescribe and describe our work environment excludes people who are more introverted." She believes leaders need to be thinking about how the workplace culture can make it safer for employees to '"the take the first step" to connect and engage with others in a more personal, more real way.

One way is encouraging an employee to participate in an ERG. Additional ways are needed.

---

5) HAVE PROGRAMS IN PLACE TO HELP EMPLOYEES STRUGGLING WITH MENTAL HEALTH ISSUES

Managers like Tom often can tell who needs to develop what skills, especially if they have been managing people for a while.

When I talked with the Dr. James Mazza, who has developed social-emotional skills curriculum for teachers to use for high school and college age students, he explained to me, "On any given day in high school or middle school, teachers are seeing about 200 kids, so they get a really good idea of what behaviors are expected" during class. So, when somebody's behaving in a way that is not expected, that seems to be problematic, teachers can identify them.

He thinks managers like Tom could do the same thing: identify what behaviors may be holding someone back. Yet he has concerns about them actually doing this.

"The thing that I worry about with managers is that they have pressure on top of them to be productive in their workplace. So, if their team doesn't accomplish a goal, if it doesn't hit a target, that looks poorly, right. So, they're going to want to push to be more efficient, which is not always effective," Mazza tells me.

This is where leaders and culture come in. If a leader is driving for a culture that values employee wellbeing, they need to train managers and reward them for helping to build a culture of wellbeing.

For example, in a company that values employee wellbeing, managers would be expected to spend time coaching their employees on behaviors they need to work on and skills they need to develop. Many even expect managers to ensure their employees have a "professional development plan."

Part of the culture of wellbeing is identifying when employees need help and providing them with the resources to get that help. Managers who recognize the signs can point them in the direction of an Employee Assistance Program, which among many other things, offers employees free confidential counseling to help with mental health concerns.

Having programs like EAP and training for managers to identify mental health signs is an important part of building a culture of wellbeing—particularly for our younger workers who may be at greater risk for mental health concerns.

REMOTE WORKERS AND CONNECTION

Laura Seredinski, an HR leader who worked for a company that was almost completely made up of remote workers, told me she had her managers do weekly thirty-minute one-on-one calls with each of their employees in order to keep them connected.

Seredinski coached her managers that they needed to be *in-tune* to what each of their employees is accountable for (their tactical accomplishments), and they also needed to be *attuned* to what's going on with each of their employees, as people. She wanted them to know how each of their employees was doing.

To get managers comfortable with this, she prescribed a form for them to use with their one-on-one calls. It instructed them to dedicate ten minutes of personal conversation.

"I think a lot of people really did use the form. It changed the connection (between manager and employee.)" Seredinski said that they had a few instances where loneliness and depression had set in with an employee and the employee opened to their managers about what they were going through. As a result, the manager was able to refer them to an Employee Assistance Program.

AM I BEING GHOSTED?

Young adults practice, or certainly many have experienced, "ghosting." Ghosting is when a personal relationship with someone, whether it be a friend or someone you are dating, is ended suddenly and without explanation by withdrawal from all communication. This means no responses to texts, and certainly not phone calls or emails.[50]

Having and handling setbacks is how we develop resilience. Being able to talk about them helps us process them faster and more fully recover. Those who "ghost" others seek to avoid the emotional upset that comes with having difficult conversations. Those who are "ghosted" can have their self-esteem drop.

Unlike a conversation, with ghosting there is no opportunity to ask questions or be provided with information that would help a person emotionally process the experience. Instead, the person is silenced and prevented from expressing emotions and being heard, which is important for maintaining self-esteem.

This practice contributes to young adults not engaging in close relationships. Without the experience that close relationships bring, young adults are not developing necessary social-emotional skills. These skills allow a person to understand, experience, express, and manage emotions and to develop meaningful relationships with others.

---

50   Vilhauer, "This Is Why Ghosting Hurts So Much."

Dr. Mazza believes managers in the workplace need to be skilled at identifying workers who are lacking social-emotional skills, the way teachers in high-school can. He would like to see workplaces and business schools offer training and courses that provide managers a baseline understanding of these skills and their importance in the workplace.

6) PROMOTE CAMARADERIE AND SAFETY ONLINE AND IRL WITH EMPLOYEES

Many iGen'ers are missing out on the social goodness that comes from in-person interactions. Pinker acknowledges that teenagers are experts at keeping track of people. She cautions that with social media, they are bringing their formative friendships from high school with them to college and to their first jobs. Because of this, she feels they are still missing out. They are not investing in deep relationships in the present moment. Instead they settle for "small digital snatches of the familiar, for hookups that don't require much emotional capital." She says their "villages are dense, intense, and interwoven but not all that local: it's now possible to be hyper-connected and extremely lonely at the same time."[51]

People spend a significant amount of time at work. At work is where social-emotional progress can be made by encouraging more in-person interaction. What's essential is that managers meet employees where they are, which often is online. They need to engage with them there in a personal and friendly way, then connect those digital conversations to in real life

---

51   Pinker, *The Village Effect: Why Face-To-Face Contact Matters*. 196-197.

conversations. In doing this, they can create a workplace culture that promotes camaraderie.

Former U.S. Surgeon General Vivek Murthy suggests managers can facilitate in-person interaction by "providing dedicated time and structured settings for people to truly get to know and understand each other. What are their values? What drives people? What are their experiences and inspirations and what are their lives outside of work?" He explains that people hunger to be known authentically.[52]

In addition to typical team-building events where you dedicate time to becoming closer as a team, a manager can foster teamwork with every interaction they have. When they interact online and in real life, they can do so in a consistent friendly manner that promotes security and nurturing.

Dr. Murthy and his team had many meetings but weren't coming together and working as a team the way he wanted. To address this, he added a five-minute agenda element to their weekly staff meetings. One person was assigned to bring in pictures of something that mattered to them and discuss the photos with the others.

"In listening, in just five minutes, we got to see whole other dimensions of people we had not understood in working together for a year," he said.

One team member turned out to be an elite runner who had qualified for the U.S. Olympic team, another team member

---

52 Picchi, "How Technology Can Lead To Loneliness In The Workplace."

shared a photo of his mother and talked about how she had been his role model. Moments of sharing stories connect us, and as Dr Murthy saw, they have tangible positive effects in the workplace.

"People started treating each other differently, stepping out of their lanes and helping each other more," Dr. Murthy says. "They felt they had been seen. It's powerful as institutions to create simple opportunities like that to see each other clearly for who they are."[53]

Each of us may not find more time in the day, but Dr. Murthy says, we can improve the quality of time we already spend together.

When managers role model this behavior, it reinforces having a healthy culture that pushes employees to develop relationship skills. Managers can help young adults find the close relationships—both at work and in their personal lives—that they need to be well to truly thrive.

Leaders,

There's a lot to know about the young adults entering the workforce. Most prominent is how, as a group, they were swiftly impacted by smartphone technology. It dramatically changed how they spent their time as teens and, as a result, how they developed. Leverage your people data in order to equip your managers. They need people data to help manage

---

[53] "The Heart Of What We Do" - Dr. Vivek Murthy On Rediscovering Meaning In Medicine."

their employees and themselves. They need education so they can be savvy with interpreting data and using data to communicate. They need training to identify those who need to develop real-life skills, and those who are struggling with mental health issues. They need to be able to build a culture that promotes camaraderie and close relationships both online and in real life. Your manager can adapt to managing in the digital revolution. Put a strategy in place to equip them with the tools, education and support they need.

ONLINE OVEREXPOSURE CAUSES DESIRE TO FEEL SAFE

In the 1980s when I was teen, I grew up interacting often out-of-view of my parents. We were in the basement, at the park, the mall, or in the backyard. Our time together was limited to our physical world. However, with a few questions or phone calls our parents could piece together who we were with, or at least get close. In the school lunchroom or study hall we had adult monitors who could, for the most part, tell what we were doing or get a sense when something wasn't right. At home, we had to get off the family phone that was tethered to the wall so someone else could use it, or simply because it was dinnertime or bedtime. When we went to our bedrooms at night, we went to sleep. We didn't have a phone or computer in our room. We were sheltered and protected.

When something traumatic happened, like a fatal car accident involving teens, chances are my parents learned about it at the same time I did. If I wasn't with them when I heard troubling news, I was at school or with some friends when I learned of the tragedy. I usually had other people with me. I was never alone with shocking, sad news.

As my sons spent more time in the digital world, first on their smartphones and later their iPads, they were spending less time in the real world. They were spending more time alone in their rooms, instead of in the kitchen or family room with the rest of us, or out with their friends at the playground or park.

iGen'ers have not been sheltered the same way I was. They have been exposed to people unknown to their parents, simply by consuming their online content or in some cases dialoguing with them in online games or chats. Many of their interactions will have had no adult monitors. No one was watching them real-time to get a sense that something wasn't right. As a result, iGen'ers have learned how to solo navigate their social interactions more so than historical teenagers, and it has stressed them out.

Not having the experience or skills to know how to handle an inflicted social injury—like the embarrassment that comes with social ridicule, amplified when hundreds of people witness it—many iGen'ers have soldiered on alone. Less than ten percent of those bullied online told an adult what happened to them. Most have witnessed others being bullied online.[54]

---

54 Pinker, *The Village Effect*. 190-191.

This has led to many iGen'ers seeking safety. They want to protect themselves against emotional upset. This concern with "emotional safety" is somewhat unique to iGen. iGen'ers work to prevent bad experiences by sidestepping situations that might be uncomfortable and avoiding people with ideas different from their own."[55]

In the workplace, expect that these employees will hold back with ideas and suggestions, or stretch assignments until they feel safe.

* * *

---

[55] Twenge, *iGen: Why Today's Super-Connected Kids Are Growing Up Less Rebellious, More Tolerant, Less Happy--And Completely Unprepared For Adulthood.* 152-153.

CHAPTER 3

BETTER THE ONLINE EMPLOYEE EXPERIENCE

Several years ago, I found myself in a beer garden near Wrigley Field on a Friday morning around 11 a.m. I had arrived there to save a table for my friends, who were joining me for the Cubs game. While I was holding the table—enjoying a cold beverage in the morning sun—I noticed that most of the others filling into the garden were men. As I watched them and listened to them, I heard several introductions being made.

"Vijay, this is Donny. Donny started that company I was telling you about. He went to college with my brother at Marquette."

"Bill, Kevin works for Quarles and Brady. He went to law school with your neighbor, Sandra."

What I realized is these people really didn't know each other well in some cases, yet they had made a commitment to spend a significant amount of time together, first at lunch then at the Cubs game.

I was impressed. These people were investing time in networking.

I decided, then and there, that I wanted to figure out a way to do the same thing—bring people together for lunch and a Cubs game with a primary purpose to introduce them and encourage them to get to know each other.

Plus, it would be fun. I loved going to Cubs games.

A few months later, my friend Shannon sent me an email sharing great news. She had gotten off the Cubs Season ticket wait list. She asked me if I wanted to "go-in" on some of her season tickets.

I took her request as a sign! I had to do this. I said, "Absolutely." Before I knew it, I was at Brownstone on Lincoln Avenue with Shannon and the other two parties she recruited, divvying up the games for the next season. I was so excited.

I decided my format would be simple. I would invite three women I knew, who didn't know each other but I thought should, to lunch and a game. At the lunch, I would have each of us share our professional stories, plus what we were working on professionally or personally and who we'd like to be networked to.

I made it happen. The day of the first game, I was nervous before everyone showed for lunch. I worried, "Would they be comfortable? Would they like each other? Would they have fun?" However, those fears evaporated once we were together. Conversation flowed, we shared, we got to know each other, and we had fun. I've been bringing women together in this way at Wrigley Field since 2012.

IGEN'ERS NOT "MEETING" AT THE BALLPARK

In 2018, in an effort to encourage my niece to embrace networking, I gave her a set of Cubs tickets for that purpose. Mary Ellen had graduated college the year before and moved to Chicago for her first job. The day after her game, we met for lunch and I asked her how it went. When she told me, "It went great." I asked her if she indeed had invited people that didn't know each other.

"Sort of."

"What do you mean?"

She told me how she knew each person. Maddie was a family friend that grew up in Michigan that she saw a couple of times a year, when their parents would get together. Elle had gone to high school with her. Kate was a friend from college.

They had all moved to Chicago after graduation and, like her, were new to the workforce. She thought they would benefit from knowing each other. Mary Ellen explained that while they had never met in person before, they had seen each other on social media since they were connected to her on Instagram and Facebook. So, they would see one another interacting with her.

For example, if Mary Ellen posted an update and one of them commented, the others would see. Through this they learned things about each other. As a result, when they got together for lunch before the game, their conversation had a head start.

ENGAGING ON SOCIAL PLATFORMS AT WORK

Matt Dodd wouldn't be surprised by Mary Ellen's comments. He has been pioneering the use of social media platforms for customer and colleague engagement for years. Matthew Dodd works for Bankwest in Perth, Western Australia, delivering their digital workplace strategy. He explains, "It is now normal to form a relationship virtually before meeting face-to-face, meaning you've already made an impression without realizing it. You can make the most of this by considering how your posts reflect who you are."[56]

Facebook and LinkedIn have "People You May Know" features. They come from things like having friends in common, being tagged in the same photo, and being from the same school, university, or work networks.[57]

Likewise, companies now need a "People You May Know" feature to encourage employees to connect digitally. Some employees have a social network, like Yammer, at their companies. What if these networks could help us out with suggestions? Perhaps suggest a social group to join based on our interests whether they be bourbon, bulldogs, or bike tours.

Yammer is like a company's "internal Facebook." You must have a working email address from your company to belong to your company's Yammer. Like Facebook, you can form groups in Yammer. Dodd says most people are consumers, versus producers, of content on Yammer since they are unsure of the medium. For this reason, he's a proponent of having fun and social groups on Yammer, like Pet Groups. This is where people post pictures of their pets and talk about their pets to each other. Plus, Dodd explains that collaboration is a learned skill but once you learn, it will become natural. You need a place to practice, and social groups are great place to start.[58]

---

[56] Dodd. "Building Trust Through Pet Pics? Are You Barking Mad?!"
[57] "Where Do People You May Know Suggestions Come From On Facebook?"
[58] Dodd. *"Building Trust Through Pet Pics?"*

ASKING QUESTIONS AND GETTING ANSWERS DIGITALLY

iGen'er Molly is in a two-year management training program with a large beer brewing company. Molly uses Salesforce every day for her job. They have an instant message feature called "chatter." There are a number of different employee groups in chatter. While she scans the messages, she's a consumer versus producer of its content. Molly tells me, "I don't honestly use it that much because you're asking a very large group of people your question. It's a little intimidating." Instead, Molly asks her questions to the group of employees that were hired with her as part of the management training group. They have created their own group message in an app called "GroupMe." It keeps this group, that is spread out across the country, digitally connected. Molly further explains that she uses text as her primary way of communicating at work. She's in the field and works out of her home. She has her phone with her constantly. She explained that she's expected to respond immediately to text messages. To me, that made sense. It's like the phone has become her proverbial "desk" and she needs to be there when her boss "walks by" with a quick question.

Using Instant Message and collaborative digital platforms, like Microsoft Teams, are catching on in many workplaces. Besides providing these platforms, leaders need to be present on them and interact with their employee there—the same as they would do in real world. Having an ongoing group chat with your team that's located in different offices should be the norm for a manager. It's how they can stay connected with warm banter, like what would happen if they could "walk around and talk" to their team members.

ENGAGING ON PUBLIC SOCIAL PLATFORMS

Most companies have a presence on social media platforms like Instagram, Twitter, and Facebook. Their employees can "meet" on those platforms too. As a leader, you can meet your employees here too. Instead of running into the newest employee at the grocery store, you now run into them on Instagram. Like at the grocery store, you can engage with them online, and as you do, you can get to know and appreciate each other.

SMARTER WORK APPLICATIONS

My niece Mary Ellen is a recruiter for her software company. As a recruiter, she works on filling close to twenty positions at a time. She reviews resumes, schedules interviews, and follows-up both with candidates and those who interview candidates. Doing her job requires manual steps including emails, instant messages, and telephone calls.

She told me that her company recently implemented a candidate tracking system. The system will integrate with a database of resumes, everyone's calendars, emails and LinkedIn. It will send automatic emails and prompts to candidates and interviewers, reminding them of tasks coming up and tasks to do, thus replacing many of Mary Ellen's manual steps. While they are still getting it completely set up, Mary Ellen likes what she has experienced so far and is positive about future enhancements. She says, "It's going to be easier to get prepared for interviews and streamline the whole process."

Mary Ellen's company clearly sees the productivity-value of integrating applications and using data to personalize employees' experiences. Whether intentional or not, what they are also doing with these operational investments is impressing their younger, more digital workers, like Mary Ellen.

NOT SMART WORK APPS

When work applications that employees use are not integrated and using people data to better the experience, employees notice. Here are two examples:

Need some software

Katie needs the software application "Snagit" added to her computer. She goes to the procurement application to order it. The procurement application does not recognize Katie. (It is not linked to the Human Resource Information System (HRIS).) It does not know her name, the office she works in, and who needs to approve her request. Katie needs to key-in this information.

If the procurement application had been integrated with the HRIS, Katie would not have had to do the extra steps of keying the information. Also, if the company had integrated their people data, they could have put some AI logic in the procurement system.[59] For example, it could prompt Katie to see if she needed other software applications (e.g. Microsoft Project, Visio) added at the same time. Since the system would know who Katie is, it would know that she is missing some applications that others in her same job have.

---

59   Artificial intelligence

Need to develop some skills
Alex wants to take an online training course. He goes to his company's learning management system (LMS) to get access to the course. The LMS does not recognize Alex (again, it is not linked HRIS). He needs to fill in information like his name, department, and cost center before he can get access to the course.

If the LMS had been integrated to the HRIS, it would have recognized Alex and he wouldn't have needed to do the extra steps of filling in the information. Also, if the company had integrated their people data, they could have put AI logic in the LMS. For example, after Alex finished the online course, it could have prompted him to rate the course and add comments about it. It could then ask him which of his colleagues he would recommend take the course—the LMS could even suggest some of the people that Alex typically interacts with.

Additionally, the LMS could suggest other courses for Alex to take based on the profiles of others that have taken the course he just completed. Along with providing the course name, the LMS could provide the course rating and comments provided by other employees, putting the comments of people in his organization on top of the list he sees.

WHAT IS IT LIKE NOW
Molly uses work applications every day. She tracks her sales activity in one system and gets marketing data needed to prepare for sales calls in another system. When I asked her what she thought about having her digital activity captured

from those applications, in order to improve what they provided her, she explained,

"I think that being in my generation—since I grew up with the Internet and everything—I don't find it creepy if it becomes more personalized. I think it would only be helpful." Then she adds, "I could see them using some AI to make it work better, more personalized."

Like Molly, most iGen'ers coming to work are comfortable working digitally and comfortable having their work-based digital data used. They will also be quick to evaluate digital experiences. When their employer is using their data to improve their digital experience, they will notice and be appreciative. When their work digital experiences are frustrating, they will notice that too, and probably share it on their group text. It will negatively impact their impression of their employer.

WHO IS WORKING-ON DIGITAL EMPLOYEE EXPERIENCES
An executive at a large SaaS company, confirmed improving employees' digital experience is already happening. "Very progressive companies are spending more time on employee (digital) engagement, but most are so consumed and trying to figure out (digital) customer engagement, so they've prioritized customers over employees because it's survival, it's growth, if they don't figure that out nothing else matters."

Ian Bailie from myHRfuture knows HR leaders at "the very progressive companies" that are spending time on employee experience (EX) in an effort to improve employee engagement. He says HR leaders need to prioritize fixing key touch points that matter in the employee journey, like those that cause friction in the experience performing infrequent tasks, like changing an address or booking a day off.

He reports that companies like IBM, EY, and Unilever are taking this on, using chatbots to assist. He explains, "Instead of having to log into the core HR system, the employee can simply use Slack, Skype (or whichever messaging tools their company uses)" to make the change."[60]

Leaders,

Make it easier for employees to meet each other, get to know each other, and work together online. Join them there to lead, converse, and encourage them. Set-up a team chat and use it for casual conversations like you would have if you were sitting in the same space. Also integrate your people data. Use it to gain insights for how to improve the employee digital experience. Start with using those insights to build-in smart AI that makes accomplishing necessary administrative tasks easier. When you do this, employees will be impressed with their company. They will stick around longer and, as a result, find more community, connection, and ways to contribute at work.

---

60 Bailee. "How Can HR Tech Help Users to Own Their Data."

CHAPTER 4
DATA PRIVACY AND ETHICS

What do you get when you put three attorneys, three data scientists, and one change management expert in a skyscraper conference room for two weeks? You get a manual process for how a global company responds to what's called a *Data Subject Access Request*—just in time for when the General Data Protection Regulation (GDPR) went into effect, on May 25, 2018.

I know that's not a funny joke. But it really was a wild, fun two weeks of my life that May. Plus, as a result, I now know a lot about the types of data companies have and the data privacy laws in place now and coming soon.

It's fascinating.

GDPR

"GDRP is the toughest privacy and security law in the world."

At its core, the legislation's stance is that people loan their information to organizations. In the regulation, these people are called "data subjects."[61]

Leaders,

These are your customers, site visitors, and your employees.

GDPR aims to give those individuals more control of that data. GDPR recognizes "privacy rights for data subjects." Included in these rights is "the right of access."

While GDPR was drafted and passed by the European Union (EU), it imposes obligations onto organizations anywhere— any organization that had data related to people in the EU.

In the case of an employee, an EU employee can ask their employer to get their personal data provided to them. The company who receives the request has a limited time to respond and additional time to comply with the request.

If a company is found in violation, there are fines. The GDPR. eu website says that "less severe infringements could result in a fine of up to €10 million, or 2% of the firm's worldwide annual revenue from the preceding financial year, whichever amount is higher."[62]

---

61   "What Is GDPR, The EU'S New Data Protection Law?"
62   "What Are The GDPR Fines?"

CCPA

On January 1, 2020 the California Consumer Privacy Act of 2018 went into effect, at least in part. This privacy law applies to employers in California that meet certain revenue thresholds or other criteria to implement policies and procedures that provide consumers—which includes employees—certain privacy rights not previously available under existing law.[63]

What is in effect now is the requirement to provide a notice to all job applicants, employees, contractors, and agents that describes how they use and disclose their personal information.

What's not in effect until January 2021 is the requirement "to honor requests for access, erasure, or opt-out from job applicants, employees, contractors, and agents with respect to personal information collected and used solely for employment purposes."[64]

LEVERAGE YOUR EFFORT—INTEGRATE YOUR PEOPLE DATA

In both cases, with GDPR and CCPA, employees can make requests for their personal data. I find this part of the whole situation most interesting.

Many expect the CCPA to be followed by a federal law around data privacy. When that happens, any employee in the USA

---

63 "Bill Text - AB-375 Privacy: Personal Information: Businesses."
64 Amodaj, et al. "Despite The Passage Of CCPA Employee Amendment, Employers Still Face Significant Compliance Burdens Under California's New Privacy Law."

can say, "Give me everything you have about me," and their employer will need to comply.

Leaders,

It's important to get in front of the privacy law requirements. See this an opportunity to not only comply with the letter of the law, but to meaningfully integrate your people data.

ETHICS

Privacy and security laws address concerns many people have about the collection and use of data. What I like about the laws is the action and transparency they insist on:

- Find your data
- Organize your data
- Secure your data, and
- Be able to show data subjects their data.

Dr. Colleen Flaherty Manchester from the Carlson School of Management, University of Minnesota thinks most employers are just trying to understand how they can use employee data for their own purpose. She sees "the biggest concern is overreach in data collection, and breach of psychological contract of trust (of the employee) with their employer" as this could undermine data collection and, more importantly, the employment relationship. Alternatively, "if the employer is seriously using it (data) to *help the employee* then maybe the employee will be less concerned about that type of data collection and data use, making it win-win as opposed to the feeling of exploitation of privacy encroachment."

I see the privacy laws driving companies to get their data organized and formulate strategies around how they will use their data, and along with this establish an understanding, a covenant between data provider and data user—or in the case of people data—employee and employer.

When this happens, even more progress can be made in using data for good.

Donncha Carroll is a partner at Axiom Partners. They provide deep analytics and decision support expertise to large companies around the world. He understands how companies are using people data today.

I discussed with him my belief that most companies have their people data spread out in various parts of the company, and many rarely look at the people data generated from operations unless there are some special circumstances like an audit or security breach.

We had been talking about how some companies use people data, including email data, to gain insights and how this concept made some people uneasy.

Carroll shared an article on workplace surveillance perceptions. It found that 73 percent of employees think their employer is likely surveilling their work activities. It found that 52.4 percent of employers surveilled work email, 39 percent surveilled Internet browser usage or history, and 38.2 percent kept tabs on in-office instant messages.[65]

---

65 "Being Watched At Work | Simplyhired"

While it is clear many companies monitor employee digital behavior, I believe the concerns that some have about companies pulling information and using it to manipulate employees is founded in fear, not fact.

When I share this with Carroll, he quips back, "For now, but it could be." Meaning, the information could certainly be used to manipulate employees in the future.

Then he adds, "It's not like every corporation is above reproach from an integrity standpoint, right? It's about the culture of the organization." That's where the real risk is.

I understand what he means. There are enough examples of bad cultures doing bad things. Enron had its leaders creating phony financials in an attempt to fool the markets. Wells Fargo created millions of fraudulent savings and checking accounts, in order for its sales leaders to cheat their way to meeting goals for bonuses.

Carroll says, "Employees are understandably concerned about how data can be used inside an organization because its utility is becoming more obvious and more valuable."

To me, this means leaders need to be on-guard for greedy, unethical people who could swoop in before proper controls are in place, and use the data to advance their own agendas at the expense of others.

One leader who understands the criticality of embedding ethics into their organization is Saleforce's CEO, Marc Benioff. In December 2018, Salesforce established an Office of Ethical and Humane Use of Technology. The office works across product, law, policy and ethics departments.

Quoted on Saleforce's website, Benioff explains "We know that technology is not inherently good or bad; it's what we do with it that matters. And that's why we're making the ethical and humane use of technology a strategic focus at Salesforce."[66]

Leaders,

Follow Benioff's lead and consider how you are weaving ethics into your company fabric when it comes to use of technology and protection of data.

Carroll is right to caution you. As you set up the capability to collect and mine employee information, make sure you mitigate the risk of unethical events happening by managing the change well. You will need to message ethics with people data use, and back it up with controls and measures. And you'll need your leaders to vigilantly monitor and hold each other to high ethical standards.

---

66 "Salesforce.com"

PART TWO

CHAPTER 5
TYPES OF PEOPLE DATA

Back in high school, I quickly learned how subjective a writing assignment could be when graded. While I enjoyed writing, I struggled with the variability of the "grade" my writing assignments would get.

Conversely, with math—no matter the teacher—the math test grades given to me always made sense. I understood the grade. There was no debate needed. My answer was either right or it was wrong.

I loved the certainty of math. Truth be told, I really needed that certainty in high school.

High school for me was a time of learning how to navigate friendships. You think you know where you stand with someone one day, then another day it would be different. Relationships are like that, especially when you are young. With experience, we learn how to be a good friend and have good friends, but it is work and sometimes unpredictable.

Certainty, I'm sure, played into why I chose to study Engineering instead of English in college. Engineering had a lot of math, and math was my reliable friend. Math didn't give you one answer one day, and another answer a different day. The answer was always the same.

USING DATA IN YOUR CASE FOR CHANGE
In my change management work, I guide leaders who are asking groups of employees to disrupt how they work and do something differently. I help the leaders see the need to provide some certainty to employees in uncertain situations.

I helped leaders of a large bank that was managing the change of shifting customers from one online banking system to another online banking system. It was a significant amount of extra work and pressure for the employees, who had to support the current system whilst learning how to support the new system.

I coached the leaders to use both words and numbers when they talked with their employees about the anticipated change. The words included the rationale for *why the change is needed* and *what it will be like* once it is over. The numbers were *the way they can know with certainty that the new way was working*.

People in change management call these numbers "the metrics." We call the overall message from the leaders "the case for change."

With the large bank moving to a new online banking system, the case for change or *why the change was needed* was that the new system worked on smartphones whereas the current system did not.

Leaders believed more customers would bank online if they could bank on their phone. A goal was established. As the number of customers who were banking online grew, leaders reported the results to employees.

When the goal was met, all involved were joyous, especially the employees who were asked to give extra effort during the transition.

People also want to know with certainty when the painful transition they are moving through is going to be "over." They can be motivated to do the extra work required of a transition and keep at it when they see that it is time-bound, has an end date, or is bound by a tangible goal. They struggle if there's no message around when the end is. Leaders need to be able to monitor and report progress toward the goal.

Having a metric and reliable data is the way to do this.

USING PEOPLE DATA TO MOTIVATE PERSONAL GROWTH
Most people are interested in information about themselves. In the old days, when I was in college, our grades were

printed and physically mailed to us through the post office. I remember going to our family mailbox daily, looking for the envelope containing my report card. I could not wait to see the new information about me. Most people when faced with cold hard facts that something isn't working, take notice. If I had a grade that disappointed me, I took notice!

Employees are interested in work information about themselves too. Having reliable data that show progress toward a personal goal helps an employee stay motivated.

The four most common types of people data that employers have are: **Wellbeing, Engagement, Performance, and Professional Development.**

For each type of people data, we'll explore:

- What it Means: Description of the data type and its primary purpose.
- Young Adults: Explain the data type related to youngest workers.
- What's Possible: Additional ways for leaders to use the information their youngest workers would appreciate.
- Do it Yourself: Suggestions for how to create and use this type of data as an individual.

In each section, we'll see how data could be presented to reassure the individual they are on the right path, or conversely motivate them to take needed action to make changes.

CHAPTER 6

WELLBEING DATA

I met a woman, Meredith, in my business networking workshop I was running at Career Transitions Center (CTC).[67] She had lost her job as an attorney in a mid-sized Chicago law firm after ten years.

When we were discussing the first set of networking practices—*meeting people*—Meredith shared a sad story with the group. She told us that she didn't get to know many people at her law firm. Her strategy had been to keep her head down and work hard, which also meant long hours.

Over the years, Meredith told herself her good work would result in recognition and a promotion, if she just worked

---

67 Name has been changed to protect privacy.

harder. She had worked so hard that she had no time for friends, not even friends at work. She explained that she'd seen the same colleagues in the halls for years and didn't even know their names.

Worse yet, Meredith seemed lonely. She spoke quietly and without emotion. When the group did *the joy exercise,* an exercise designed to provide people ideas of where they could meet people, Meredith was not able to come up with one activity that brought her joy. Her job had been her life, and now her job was over.

Jillian Richardson, author of *Unlonely Planet,* knows the value of using joy to meet people. When she moved to New York City, she was lonely. She recognized others must have the challenge of meeting people in NYC too. So, she started The Joy List. It's a weekly newsletter of events that New Yorkers can go to by themselves and leave with a new friend. Her mission is to make New York City less lonely.[68]

Meredith needed–a joy list. Perhaps with that in hand, she would give herself permission to take time for developing meaningful relationships.

As hard as they can be, relationships of all types—be they romantic or friendships, with family members or neighbors, with co-workers or managers—give us experiences that challenge and make us grow. They can inspire us, calm us down, and lift us up.

---

68 Richardson. "Opinion | What America's Loneliest Generation Suggests About Modern Interaction."

WELLBEING DATA

My hope is that many employers will begin making it an employee requirement to work on social skills and related practices that lead to camaraderie at work, better performance, and joy in their personal lives.

Many employers are taking steps in the right direction. For example, they provide for their employees an online health assessment.

Wellbeing data is generated from survey "health assessments."

A health assessment is a questionnaire that evaluates health risks and quality of life. It usually has three key elements: the questionnaire, a risk calculator or score, and some form of feedback (usually an automatic online report). Sometimes the feedback is a conversation with a health advisor. The feedback often provides recommendations on how individuals can reduce their health risks by changing their lifestyle.

Many large employers use Health Assessments and partner with wellbeing vendors, like Virgin Pulse or Limeade, to administer these and other wellbeing programs.

I spoke with Andre Burkholder, director of health management at Willis Towers Watson. We talked about how many employers are measuring more than just physical health, they also now measure overall wellbeing. Wellbeing in this context is the experience of health, happiness, and prosperity.[69] Willis Towers Watson's wellbeing definition includes physical, emotional social, and financial dimensions, as shown below.

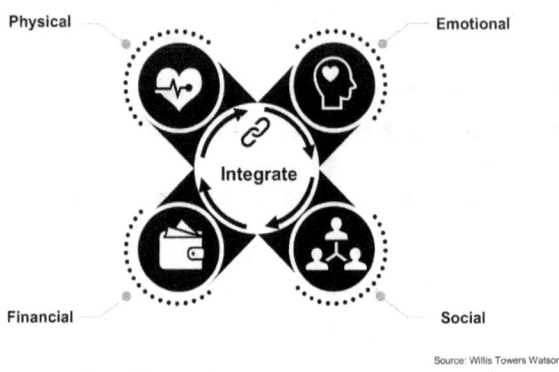

Source: © Willis Towers Watson 2020. All rights reserved. Reprinted with permission.

WELLBEING DATA—YOUNG ADULTS

The emotional dimension of wellbeing programs has been getting significant attention recently. This is due in part to the fact that mental illnesses have risen "dramatically" worldwide in the past twenty-five years. Roughly one billion of the

---

69   Aldana. *What Is Wellness? With No Wellness Program Definition It's Everything.*

3.4 billion working adults globally suffer from anxiety, and one in four experience a mental disorder.[70]

Anxiety is the most common mental health disorder in the U.S. It has been the most common reason college students seek counseling services. A college association reported that 62 percent in 2016 of undergraduates reported "overwhelming anxiety" up from 50 percent in 2011. Throughout the mental health community, other data is showing this same sharp rise.[71]

When did this start and why? Jean M. Twenge, expert on generational differences in American youth, can tell you why.[72]

Twenge has been analyzing generational differences for twenty-five years. She has looked at generational data from as far back as the 1930s. She explains that usually "the characteristics that come to define a generation appear gradually." As they appear, they wash out the characteristics of the generation before them.

In 2012, Twenge was shocked to see data for the iGen'ers that looked like nothing she had ever seen before. As she looked at the latest data on beliefs and behaviors of American teens, she didn't see the gradual soft indications of changes in the beliefs and behaviors from the previous generation

---

70 Williams, "Power To The People: The Changing Face of Employee Well-being."
71 Denizet-Lewis. "Why Are More American Teenagers Than Ever Suffering From Severe Anxiety?"
72 Twenge, "Have Smartphones Destroyed A Generation?"

(Millennials). Instead the data was a hard, loud cry: "We are different."

Again, this group is those born between 1995 and 2012, whom Twenge calls iGen. The first from this group will have their twenty-fifth birthday in 2020.

Twenge says the abrupt shifts are somewhat due to differences in their worldviews and mostly in how they spend their time. What happened in 2012 that caused such dramatic shifts in behavior is that this was the moment when the proportion of Americans who owned a smartphone surpassed fifty percent, according to Twenge's research.

The arrival of the smartphone radically changed every aspect of iGen's lives. The experiences iGen'ers have every day are different from those of the generation that came of age just a few years before them. This includes the nature of their social interactions and their mental health. Twenge states this generation is on the brink of the worst mental-health crisis in decades.

Her research reveals that "the twin rise of the smartphone and social media has caused an earthquake of a magnitude we've not seen in a very long time, if ever." She continues, "There is compelling evidence that the devices we've placed in young people's hands are having profound effects on their lives—and are making them seriously unhappy."[73]

---

73 Ibid.

WHAT'S POSSIBLE

So many people love their Fitbits. Fitbit is the wearable technology device that measures data such as steps walked, heart rate, and sleep quality. Lately, I hear someone reference the Fitbit almost every day. Perhaps that's because there are twenty-seven million active Fitbit users.[74]

Their obsession with Fitbit proves to me that there's an interest in wellbeing data. I think most of the Fitbit users would agree—engaging with data about your wellbeing is fun.

Some companies are starting to provide wellbeing data through smartphones, but not many. LifeWorks, who offers this service, did a study in 2018 that showed while only less than five percent of those surveyed could access their wellbeing services through a smartphone, more that seventy-five percent of respondents expressed a desire to access these services from any place at any time.[75]

There is demand for more accessible experience that fits with our technology-driven life.

Employees could have their wellbeing data presented to them in an app that is engaging and interactive. I imagine a dashboard with graphs, charts, and tables that you could interact with to better understand the information. I'd also see you being able to both set goals and monitor progress toward those goals with updated data. Plus, having a social element

---

74 Lui. "Fitbit - Statistics & Facts." Technology & Telecommunications.
75 "Employees Want To Take Control Of Their Wellbeing With Mobile Access To Services."

would be key to let you applaud your friends' accomplishments and share your latest results.

For a more complete picture, we could add other wellbeing datasets to it, like our medical records. Anyone can now get their medical records electronically.

Employees could have their wellbeing data integrated with their other personal work data in order to gain insights.

Burkholder explains that right now the huge trend in the industry is for wellbeing vendors to help people navigate to the right benefit resource at the right time. I took this to mean that if they appear to have a risk of heart disease, they can connect to information that will encourage them to get help.

He went on to explain to me that which vendor a company uses and how they partner with them depends on the company's wellbeing strategy. For example, perhaps the company had a strategy to encourage specific behavior changes of their employees, like quitting tobacco or not consuming too much alcohol. In this case, they would work with a vendor who has a way to address those goals.

I wondered about individual employees' goals.

I told Burkholder I liked the four dimensions of the Willis Towers Watson wellbeing point of view. I shared the thesis of providing employees an engaging, interactive dashboard of their people data with him. I asked him if companies today were serving up to employees their wellbeing data in a format where they can compare it and see progress?

He said some vendors do provide an employee dashboard where they could see a lot of different things related to their wellbeing metrics. However, more often what happens is an employer gets access to aggregate reports that show overall progression of data. However, he thinks employees could benefit from seeing the progression of their personal data too.

Burkholder added that, "Vendors don't do a good enough job showing the actual user (employee) if they're improving." He thinks this is a huge "gap in the industry."

Leaders,

You invest in collecting data about your employees' wellbeing annually. Leverage that investment by using the data for more.

☐ Work with a wellbeing vendor to ensure wellbeing data is put in front of each employee in an engaging way, like a dashboard, that encourages them to set goals, monitor progress, and improve wellbeing.
☐ Analyze the aggregate company-wide results to show how, as an organization, many are working toward improving their wellbeing.
☐ Solicit volunteers to share the story of their wellbeing journey.
☐ Promote the progress the organization is making by using employee testimonials of people making strides toward improving their overall wellbeing.

DO IT YOURSELF

If your organization does not measure your wellbeing or have a wellbeing program, consider these actions to embrace measuring and improving your wellbeing:

- ☐ Set goals. Dr. Timothy Long is the Chief Clinical Officer at Alliance Chicago and Health Choice Network/ Miami. He suggests meeting with a primary care doctor for an overall wellbeing check. During your visit, you agree on one, two, or three wellbeing goals. Schedule a follow-up appointment with your primary care doctor to check on progress.
- ☐ Get an accountability partner. Enlist the support of a friend to encourage you. Perhaps someone you believe does a good job with managing their wellbeing. Share your goals with them.
- ☐ Track your activities. Some services send text messaging such as, "Did you pick up your anti-hypertension medicine?" that prompt people to stay on the right path toward better overall wellness. Set up your own alerts or reminders on your calendar for critical tasks such taking medicine, exercise, or setting up coffee to reconnect with a friend.

CHAPTER 7
ENGAGEMENT DATA

In 1988, I worked at Dolores Mission, the poorest parish in Los Angeles at that time. Greg Boyle, S.J. (Father G) was the pastor there. He was new to being a Jesuit, and I was new to being an adult. While I was teaching sixth, seventh, and eighth graders in the East L.A. neighborhood notorious for vicious gangs, Father G was beginning his outreach to gang members.

Over thirty years later, his good work has evolved into Homeboy Industries, a company he founded. It is the largest and most successful gang intervention, rehabilitation, and job re-entry program in the world. They currently employ over

200 high-risk, formerly gang-involved, and recently incarcerated youth.[76]

Additionally, Father G speaks around the world to inspire others to consider the principles he and his team use for their work.

Provide kinship—We are all in need of kinship.

When former gang members were solely provided with a job, many returned to the gangs. When Homeboy Industries studied this phenomenon, they concluded that in addition to a job, they needed to provide former gang members with counseling and a consistent, supportive culture. When they did this, most gang members were able to stay away from the gangs. Culture matters. Invest in your culture and keep an eye on it.

Practice extravagant tenderness—We all need to be understood.

When former gang members experienced compassion from Homeboy Industries, they were able to identify and address what caused them to join gangs. By being part of the Homeboy Industries family, they were able to see sympathetic behavior role-modeled, and as a result become sympathetic and compassionate with others. When people on your team endure extraordinary personal hardship, be there for them. Offer support that you think would be helpful if you were they. Encourage others to do the same.

---

76 "Homeboy Industries.com."

***Promote hope**—We can feel hopeless when we don't know what's ahead.*

Homeboy Industries counseling provides former gang members an eighteen-month road map to a gang-free life. Plus, Homeboy Industries' employees include rehabilitated gang members. Gang members in the program are able to get to know others who have already transformed.

When Homeboys Industries focused on culture, their success-rate soared. This is in large part due to the culture of safety and openness that Father G has established and vigilantly maintains. Homeboy Industries has become a model for other organizations in cities around the world.

ENGAGEMENT DATA

Daniel Coyle has studied highly successful groups that have defied odds, not unlike Homeboy Industries has.

In his book, *The Culture Code,* he poses the question, "Why do certain groups add up to become greater than the sum of their parts, while others add up to be less?" What his three years of research has yielded is the same thing Father G figured out: it's about creating and sustaining a great culture.

Coyle explains, "Group Culture is one of the most powerful forces on the planet. We sense its presence inside successful businesses, championship teams, and thriving families, and we sense when it's absent or toxic."[77]

---

77 Coyle. *The Culture Code.*

While you can sense it, having a way to measure your culture both helps drive action for addressing issues and seeing if the solutions you implemented worked. Many companies use "employee engagement" as their metric when they are working to improve their cultures.

Forbes describes employee engagement as "the emotional commitment the employee has to the organization and its goals."[78] The most common way to measure employee engagement is surveys. Other ways include one-on-one meetings and interviews, and something called the employee Net Promoter score (eNPS). eNPS is touted as one of the most effective and simple ways to measure engagement. It is one question that truly gauges loyalty. For example, while you may be satisfied in your job, would you recommend your company as a good place to work? Would you recommend the products/services they sell?[79]

Engagement data is generated from the instruments that measure "employee engagement."

Royal Rarick has worked on employee engagement surveys for clients of a large Human Resources consulting firm. He explained to me that it's commonly believed that when a company's employees are "engaged," the company performs better. He told me some employers have been measuring engagement with surveys for decades. He says the process is pretty straight forward:

---

78 Kruse. "What Is Employee Engagement."
79 Robins. "How To Properly Measure Employee Engagement."

1. Employees are surveyed with questions that measure levels of engagement across many factors. Employers pose questions that dig into why or why not groups of employees are engaged.
2. Then the data is served up to the leaders via an online reporting tool that has charts, tables, and graphs.
3. He explains, "The online reporting technology recently has become much more affordable and easier to set up."
4. Managers can pop into their tool and compare anything they want, any time.

A typical engagement survey will ask questions with an agreement scale such as Agree/Tend to Agree/Neutral/Tend to Disagree/Disagree. Here's a sample of questions that represent what is typical.[80]

- I understand the strategic goals of the company.
- I see a clear link between my work and the company's goals and objectives.
- I am proud to be a member of my team.
- When something unexpected comes up in my work, I know who to ask for help.
- I receive the appropriate training needed to do my job.
- I receive the support and information from my manager that I need.
- My manager is a great role model for employees.
- I have the work-life balance I need.
- I believe there are good career opportunities for me at this company.

---

80 Croswell. "20 Simple Employee Engagement Survey Questions You Should Ask."

- I see myself still working here in two years' time.

Rarick explains that after the results of an engagement survey are reviewed by management, sometimes further information will be desired.

- For example, if a specific team within an organization shows very high engagement results, they may be interviewed to understand what practices are happening that could be used by other teams.
- Conversely, if a team has a lower score in one area like, "When something unexpected comes up in my work, I know who to ask for help," a follow-up survey to this group may solicit examples and details in order to better address the situation.

An executive at a large SaaS company told me they do employee surveys twice a year. They look at their results and benchmark how people are progressing. They want to know how engaged employees really are. The leader explains the twice a year surveying: "We do lots of things around employee engagement because our whole belief is employees who are fully engaged and committed, do better work."

ENGAGEMENT DATA—YOUNG ADULTS

Generational research is indicating that the youngest workers will be seeking engagement but won't be easily engaged.

The root cause of this has to do with something called psychological safety. The phrase was coined by Amy Edmondson, an organizational behavioral scientist. She defined it as "a shared belief held by members of a team that the team is safe for interpersonal risk-taking." She further describes it as "a team climate characterized by interpersonal trust and mutual respect in which people are comfortable being themselves" [81]

Google's Project Aristotle resulted in people learning about psychological safety. They did hundreds of interviews and analyzed data taken from over one hundred active teams at Google. What they found was above all else, psychological safety was crucial to ensuring that a team works well together. Feeling psychologically secure, safe, and all right being vulnerable is not something many younger workers are bringing with them to work. Research shows that many of them have **not** had enough experiences in adolescence to build these essential skills. In fact, for many young adults these skill gaps are contributing to anxiety and in extreme cases suicide attempts. Many believe we are on the brink of a generational health crisis.

IPADS AND PSYCHOLOGICAL SAFETY

I am the parent of two young adults, and while researching this book I have felt pangs of regret. As I interpreted the research, it has become clear to me that a key contributor to the potential health crisis is a lapse in parenting. Beginning in 2012, many of us parents were putting smartphones in the hands of our pre-teens and teens.[82]

---

81 "Psychological Safety Defined."
82 Twenge, *Have Smartphones Destroyed a Generation?*

As I reflect on it, it's actually embarrassing to think about how it went down. My story is, "Well, everyone was getting their kids smartphones. No one knew it was bad. I didn't want my sons to miss out. I didn't want them to be left behind their peers."

It seems laughable now.

The truth is I was caught up in the excitement of the new technology. Of course, I had gotten myself a smartphone too, and we were all having fun with them. I didn't want to consider that perhaps it was not a good idea to let your child have unsupervised access to the Internet and all that comes with it—pornography, bad role models, and negative influencers. I left my sons unsupervised on the digital playground. When they were online on their phones, I wasn't there and no one else they knew really was there with them on their phones either. What they experienced in the digital world—be it joyous or troubling—they experienced alone.

Up until then, most of the time if one of my sons experienced something like a sad story from a neighbor, a rude person at the park, or a violent TV scene, I experienced it with them. If I wasn't there, most likely a caregiver, teacher, coach, or another parent was there or close by. They would let me know what happened. Then my son and I could talk about it. I could answer his questions. I could provide my perspective—I could re-assure him.

As my sons spent more time in the digital world, first on their smartphones and later on their iPads, they were spending less time in the real world. They were spending more time physically alone in their rooms instead of in the kitchen or family room with the rest of us or out with their friends at the playground or the park.

I remember in the beginning my husband John was hesitant to give our sons smartphones. I talked him into it.

When our oldest son started high school in 2013, iPads were being rolled out. The school held an information session with parents to discuss it. One father asked if the iPads would have access to the "whole" Internet.

Some of us snickered smugly thinking, "This poor soul doesn't understand the brave new world." When the school administrator said yes, the father looked stricken. He, like John, was right to be concerned. Sadly, voices like theirs were drowned out by those of us enamored with our shiny new phones. [83]

I was excited to learn together with my sons how to use them: how to email from your phone, put "likes" on Facebook posts, send text messages, and later use Instagram and Twitter. Since my sons dove right in and figured it out, John and I quickly handed over the reins of household technology and the digital world to them.

We asked them our tech questions, and they knew the answers or quickly figured them out. It gave us something new talk to them about. It was fun.

---

83 Since iPads were first introduced in schools, many schools have instituted rules that protect the student experience including the high school our sons attended.

The truth is, I was having so much fun that I took my eye off the ball. I regret that I didn't have the courage to be the outlier parent and say to our sons, "This is wrong. I will not allow you unrestricted access to the Internet."

I wish I had been the parent that had gone against the grain and listened to my conscience.

Bella's group chat

Bella, who is twelve years old, knows parents that are going against the grain. She told me that her class has a group chat that she participates in from her iPad mini.

She said it had become her alarm clock and most days was going off too early for her. I asked her to explain. She said that around 6:30 a.m., sometimes earlier, the "ping" that let her know a text has been sent would sound. While she would try to ignore it, soon there were would inevitably be several other "pings"—so many that it was like a "wake-up song." She went on to say that she figured out how to "silence the chat" since she likes to wake up later.

I asked her if everyone from her class was in the chat. She first said yes. Then I questioned, "Does everyone have an iPad or smartphone?" She said, "Almost everyone—one of the girls doesn't, Audrey."

She went on to say that Audrey's family doesn't let them have iPads, smartphones, or gaming systems until they turn eighteen. Her brother, Sean, had just turned eighteen and "He got a smartphone and a gaming system for his birthday!"

I asked if it was hard for Audrey not having an iPad mini or smartphone. Bella said, "Not really, we just need to remember to tell her our plans." I asked what is Audrey like? She said "She's great. She's always doing things—fun things like getting us together to go the park or the bagel shop."

Safe Village

Bella and her friends are forming what Susan Pinker calls "a village." In her book, *The Village Effect*, she describes a village as a "tight knit group of friends and family in our corner, and not just when the chips are down."

Pinker spent three years delving into the fairly new field of social neuroscience. What she learned is that we need more than digital villages, we need villages that interact face-to-face. She explains, "If we don't interact regularly with people face to face, the odds are we won't live as long, remember information as well, or be as happy as we could have been."[84]

BEING ONLINE CHANGED HOW TEENS DEVELOPED

Jean Twenge's research also found that we need more than digital villages. She published a study showing that, "Teens whose face time with friends is mostly on their phones are the loneliest of all, but even those who mix real-world socializing with social media still are increasingly isolated."[85]

---

84 Pinker, *The Village Effect: Why Face-To-Face Contact Matters*. 4.
85 O'Donnell. "Teens Aren't Socializing in the Real World. And That's Making Them Super Lonely."

As I studied the research, I reflected and wondered about what is going on. Where I've landed is that this generation has suffered emotional ups and downs differently than those of us who came of age before smartphones were attached to our hands.

Many have experienced a lot of harsh news, both personal and public news, alone with their eyes glued to the screen of the phone in their hand. Hour after hour, day after day, they are having intense digital experiences. They don't turn away.

Experts have shown some of the technology was designed to be addicting, to get people to spend more time on the applications. Evidence is showing the design features worked. Tech profits have increased. The cost left out of the business case was the degraded health of our youngest, most vulnerable users.

As a result, these youths have a strong need to "protect against emotional upset" and are "concerned with emotional safety."

How this looks:

- They seek to prevent bad experiences.
- They sidestep situations that might be uncomfortable.
- They avoid people with ideas different from their own.
- They are lonely.[86]

---

[86] "iGen Quotes By Jean M. Twenge."

NEEDING TO FEEL SAFE LEADS TO NEEDING TO BE PERFECT

Some are coping by seeking to control by striving for perfection. Perfectionism is the desire to produce work or perform at high standards. Research says around forty percent of young adults are exhibiting perfectionist tendencies.

"For perfectionists, any failure to meet such expectations can cause them to feel frustrated or angry or even that they can "never be good enough"—often leading them to "quit the field;" and worse, perfectionism is linked to the development of conditions like depression, anxiety, eating disorders, and self-harm and it is linked to suicide.[87]

Because of the digital relationships and experiences during their youth, the youngest workers may not seek out close relationships at work or become easily engaged in the mission of their company. Also, they may not share their ideas freely with co-workers the way necessary to get the most from collaboration. This is the case unless, of course, there are special tactics to address the skills they need to develop in order to find their safe village at work.

TECHNOLOGY

While it may not sound like it, I actually do like technology. I have changed some of my habits in response to one of Cal

---

87 "40% Of Young Adults Exhibit Perfectionist Tendencies – It's Not Good!"

Newport's messages: "Make technology *work* for you. Don't *work* for technology," but I still am enamored with my smartphone, my laptop and television.[88]

Most iGen'ers would agree smartphones and technology work for them too and going tech-free is not an option they would consider. One iGen'er pointed out to me that being active digitally has social benefits. He says prohibiting tech-use for children is not the answer.

He explains, "While smartphones may hinder conversation with people your generation and older (i.e. those who did not grow up with smartphones). This is not the case with me and my peers. With my generation, everyone talks about what goes on in social media, the latest video game, or the newest show on Netflix. By withholding technology from kids, you are making kids less social, because they cannot talk about what their friends are talking about."

In the workplace it is the same—employees are working online, and they talk about those experiences.

Leaders,

The online experience matters. Purposely improve your employees' online experience. When you do, it will strengthen your employees' emotional commitment to your organization and its goals. Have your engagement data tell the story, that when young workers join your company, they indicate that they "see themselves still working there in two years' time."

---

88 Newport, *Avoiding Digital Distraction.*

WHAT'S POSSIBLE

Putting engagement data into the hands of the employee is possible. The employee could see what part of their experience at work is not working for them—be it their current role, their manager, or work-life balance. They could see the engagement results of others in their organization and compare.

Also, when an employee has low scores, they could be presented with a complete a series of behavioral questions that could present skills that may be hindering their engagement. As a result, they could be offered suggestions to learn how to address their problems.

In-person Dialogues

An executive, whose company brings in around a hundred college interns, told me that they realized the interns needed training on how to have phone conversations. A leader in another organization said in a discussion with a group of college interns, one told the group she was petrified of having an in-person meeting where she was expected to talk one-on-one. The other interns expressed the same angst.

Non-verbal Communication

Sanjay Kirtikar, a technology executive with over twenty years of experience managing IT employees says, "Social media is ruining social skills." His observation is that workers seem to be struggling with having productive verbal conversations at work. Research backs-up Kirtikar's claim. It shows that many are more comfortable communicating via words and emojis on their phones than face-to-face with words from their mouth. They know the right emoji to use in a text, but don't always know the right facial expression to use, which of course means they don't know how to read those facial expressions as well, either.[89]

Done right, an engagement survey could probe to find if the root cause of a disengaged employee is related to a specific skill gap—be it comfort with telephone conversations or face-to-face contact. Then, offer suggestions for how to address.

Leaders,

Leverage your engagement data to uncover the individuals who are struggling with engagement because of weaknesses in some behavioral skills. Show them their engagement data, along with questions that unearth what else might be going on personally that's causing them to hold back in the workplace. When you do, you will ignite in them the desire to develop skills needed and a desire to continue being a part of a company that cares about them.

---

89 Pinker, *The Village Effect: Why Face-To-Face Contact Matters.* 90-91

DO IT YOURSELF

To determine if you are engaged, consider this list of "Signs you are in the **right** job even if it doesn't feel like it" from Áine Caine.

Check the boxes that apply to you.[90]

- ☐ Time flies at work—you are having fun.
- ☐ You challenge yourself and take risks—you are encouraged to experiment and test the limits.
- ☐ You don't need coffee every morning—your energy comes from the cool work you get to do.
- ☐ Your boss pushes you to strive for more.
- ☐ Your coworkers are more like friends and the people you work with are really a team.
- ☐ You have enough time for loved ones and yourself.
- ☐ You're calm on Sundays. You don't feel dread or sadness.
- ☐ You're annoying on Mondays. That is, you're annoyingly positive because you are happy to be at work.
- ☐ You never shut up about work because you like sharing what you are up to.
- ☐ Your organization is doing well and isn't dying a swift, bitter death.
- ☐ You're fine with necessary, mundane tasks—once done you get back to what you love.
- ☐ Money's not an issue. Your pay is awesome and reflects what you bring to the organization.
- ☐ You want your boss's job and feel well-suited for an upward trajectory at your company.

---

90 Caine. "13 Signs You're In The Right Job, Even If It Doesn't Feel Like It."

If you have an unchecked box, determine what action you can take to remedy the situation. Discuss this exercise with a trusted friend.

If there are several unchecked boxes, follow the advice of Tony Hsieh, entrepreneur, venture capitalist and author and go "sit at a different table." Go find somewhere else to work, where your awesomeness is appreciated.[91]

---

91   Bradt. "Be Like Zappos' Tony Hsieh - Answer Three Key Onboarding Due Diligence Questions."

CHAPTER 8
PERFORMANCE DATA

I like to be on-time. I am pretty much early for everything. One sunny summer morning, I was thirty minutes early for a meeting at the Mart in Chicago. I decided to get some tea in a nearby cafe on Kinzie Street.

As I was sitting at the bar of the cafe enjoying my tea, I noticed a man dressed in shirtsleeves and a tie push a stroller into the cafe. While he was in the queue to place his order, I heard a sweet little voice from the stroller say, "Wa-wa." The man turned to the toddler and said, "You would like some water?" to which the little voice responded, "Wa-wa."

"Okay Ruby. I'll get you some water." The man replied.

Then the man placed his coffee order. After which he pushed the stroller toward the end of the bar where the jug of water was sitting.

"Wa-wa."

"I'm getting you some water Ruby."

"Wa-wa."

"Yes Ruby, I know you want some water. Here you go." He handed her a sippy cup of water.

A few seconds later I hear, "You have to leave the top on Ruby, or you can't have it." Ten seconds later I heard a cry.

"Waaaaaaaaaaaaaaaaaaaaaaaaa!"

"Do you want it back?"

"Wa-wa!"

"Then you have to keep the top on."

Silence.

Then the man pushed the stroller toward the door of the café, and left.

I'm struck by the interaction. It both amused me and warmed my heart. Like Ruby, most of us need reassurance that we are heard. Like Ruby, most of us have tested the limits of a rule or two.

PERFORMANCE DATA

In the workplace, performance data is generated in numerous ways—it can be an annual event or more frequent. It is a measure of how an employee is performing at their job. It is usually conducted by the employee's manager. It is meant to both reassure an employee that they are performing well and provide knowledge when they not performing as required.

> **Performance data is the information collected related to an employees' job performance. It shows how well they are complying with the job's established expectations. It can also be information that shows an employee has been coached on how to perform better.**

PERFORMANCE DATA—COACHING

It can be exhausting to respond to someone's needs and their need to be heard. Yet the effort is not in vain. In a *Harvard Business Review* article by communication researchers, Jack Zenger and Joseph Folkman, they point out that—like a trampoline does for a child—good listening provides "energy, acceleration, height and amplification" to the person being heard.[92]

---

[92] Zenger and Folkman. "What Great Listeners Actually Do."

Like Ruby, I have a dad that is a good listener. Often after talking with my dad, I feel like I've been on a trampoline. I'm happier, more positive, and confident. One time in college, I was preparing to deliver a speech about process improvement. I knew several of the other students were going to use impressive examples from their summer internships. I didn't have an example like that. I decided to share an example of how I was able to get one of my house mates, Stephanie, to make her breakfast faster so she would not be tempted to skip breakfast.

As the day of my presentation got closer, I was regretting my choice. I talked to my dad to express my fear that the professor and other students would laugh at my unimpressive example. My dad listened and, as he did, asked me questions and took my concerns seriously. As we continued to converse, he laughed as I shared the story of how I got Stephanie organized so she could shave four minutes off her ten-minute breakfast preparation. Then I laughed too. He told me I was going to have fun giving the presentation and everyone was going to enjoy it. The conversation with my dad had reassured me and my speech went well.

In *The Village*, Susan Pinker provides impressive research that demonstrates that face-to-face contact conversations make us healthier and happier. Conversations with someone you trust when you are struggling with something helps you see more clearly and think through what you need to do. Conversations in the workplace can do the same. Often those work conversations are between you and your manager, and they are about how you as an employee are performing.[93]

When I worked at American Express in operations, the culture was all about "excellence." People prided themselves on doing excellent work. Leaders were always talking about excellence and quality.

Every process in operations had standards and were measured. Also, individuals who were part of those processes had goals and their performance was measured and provided to them frequently.

The operations area I worked in was called a Payment Center. A long time ago, most credit card companies like American Express physically mailed a paper statement to cardholders each month that told them how much money was due. The payment center was where the customers then mailed their credit card payments.

Each person who was part of these operations had a timeliness goal: how fast they need to do their step in the process.[94] Each person knew their performance goals and would get their results often. Teams of employees have performance goals too. The results of their team were compared to other teams by being put on a board so everyone could see them. They were read out loud daily by the shift manager in team meetings. Individual performers who excelled were pointed out in team meetings too. There was great pride in your team

---

93 Pinker, *The Village Effect: Why Face-To-Face Contact Matters.*
94 Each person had a quality goal too and it was the same—100 percent quality.

having the best performance. There was great pride in having, meeting, and exceeding personal performance goals too.

Having the hard facts of performance data made all this possible. In the workplace, many functions have standards and having messages from leaders that clearly articulate both what's expected and what's inspected is key to driving a culture that cares about performance.

PERFORMANCE DATA—COMPLIANCE
Ruby's dad let her know that the lid needed to stay on the sippy cup of water, or she could not have it. When she didn't heed his direction, he took the cup back.

As a parent, conscious or not, you pick what behaviors you are going to model and promote with your child. Then (at least for this parent) there's a sub-set of those behaviors that you consistently enforce. For most parents, it is simply impossible and exhausting to enforce all of them. (Thank goodness for others like relatives, neighbors, friends, teachers, and coaches that also help with the re-enforcing.)

While we try to exemplify everything we care about—our personal values drive our selection of what we actually consistently enforce. This set of values defines to the child what is important to their parent.

In our family, one of the behaviors I expect is the writing of thank you notes. Once my son could hold a crayon, I worked with him to acknowledge his gratitude each and every time he received a gift, by giving a note to the giver.

His brother joined the thank you note activity too, when he was old enough. Each boy having their own stationery for this purpose was eventually added to the ritual, as was a return address stamp.[95]

As a leader, what you model and enforce is noted by your workforce.

When I was a consultant, there was an organization I worked for that popped-up a message on my screen every time I selected the command to print something in color, asking me to consider printing it in black and white instead. I had to click the screen acknowledging I saw the message for the print command to be executed. I am sure the pop-up changed my behavior sometimes. If I had been given some data about my printer usage relative to a standard, my guess is my behavior would have changed even more. Without this standard and measurement against it, I was left to determine if my behavior was with normal limits.

When I worked at American Express, it became known that some employees were looking up famous peoples' credit card information because they were curious about what they were purchasing and liked to share the interesting information with their family and friends.

This resulted in the company establishing a quarterly practice of providing each employee a piece of paper (this was,

---

[95] I knew this habit was getting ingrained each time one son would remind me that the other son, who had received a gift, needed to write a thank you note. As their Grandma Louise would say, "That was an example of 'brotherly-love.'"

of course, the early 90s) to sign acknowledging that we each knew it was against company policies to look up customer information, unless it was necessary for our respective jobs. No one can be sure how well this worked, since at the time the technology available did not allow an employer to trace which screens an employee viewed. But suffice it to say, the message was clear: if you don't comply, you will lose your job.

Later, when I worked for a regional bank in the early 2000s, each employee who had a computer was presented with a screen when they turned on his or her computer. It said something like, "We are watching your activities and if you do anything against bank policies, you will face disciplinary action that could include termination."

We had to click the box acknowledging that we had seen this message.

This was around the time that employers were cracking down on employees using their work computers for viewing pornography, gambling, and sending inappropriate emails. I remember several chain emails being passed around, and that was banned too. Just about everyone I knew in the corporate world knew someone who lost their job because of being caught using company computers inappropriately.

Changing your behavior can be hard. It's also difficult to assess whether it's really necessary without guidance, policies, and performance data. As a leader, you need to make clear what's expected of your employees and how they are doing. Use performance data to do this.

PERFORMANCE DATA—YOUNG ADULTS

When I first started working in Chicago, I lived in the Lincoln Park neighborhood on the Northside. It was a mix of modest apartment rental buildings like mine and stunning multi-million-dollar homes. As I walked the quarter mile each morning to the Fullerton train stop, I'd amuse myself by deciding which house I would buy, if I could.

I usually traded off between three of the beautiful homes I passed. Then, at some point I started buying a weekly lottery ticket. I reasoned it gave me a chance to get my dream home sooner. Each week, I would buy the ticket and before the drawing, I'd have the home picked out that I would buy should I win the lottery the next day. Then I'd check after the drawing to see if I won. This went on for several months.

Addiction and Dopamine

What started to happen was each week I would find myself getting excited about moving out of my dumpy apartment with no air conditioning and chipping paint on the walls and into a new, beautiful home.

Addiction researcher Mike Robinson explains this is because dopamine—the happy neurotransmitter the brain releases during enjoyable activities—is also released during the moments leading up to a potential reward, like when I was dreaming about my new home.[96]

[96]

Counterintuitively, in individuals with a gambling problem, losing also triggers the rewarding release of dopamine almost to the same degree that winning does. "As a result, in problem gamblers, losing sets off the urge to keep playing, rather than the disappointment that might prompt you to walk away," says Robinson. This is called *the slot machine effect* after the casino game of the same name.[97]

Luckily at some point, I realized buying a lottery ticket and thinking I could actually win and then feeling down when I didn't, was consuming too much of my time and I needed to stop. So, I stopped. I must admit, at first, I did miss having the weekly thrill. Reflecting on this gives me a small insight into addiction and dopamine.

Social Approval Addiction

Another activity that's taking time away from people is addictive technology like Facebook, Twitter, and Instagram. According to Cal Newport, associate professor of Computer Science at Georgetown and author of *Digital Minimalism*, the average modern user spends around two hours per day on social media and related messaging services and compulsively checks their devices around eighty-five times per day.[98]

Newport explains that human brains have evolved to take part in very complex and subtle social processes. Our evolved brain is what has allowed humans to thrive so much. We are very good at monitoring people around us. We monitor

---

97 Robinson. "How Gambling Distorts Reality And Hooks Your Brain."
98 Newport. *Digital Minimalism: Choosing A Focused Life In A Noisy World.* 6

people's opinions of us and navigate complex interactions to see where we are in a particular social interaction according to tribal hierarchy. Our brain does this really well. Knowing this, experts at Facebook set out to design new features to take advantage of these social tendencies.

Newport reports that they changed the social media experience from a static one, where people were posting photos and status updates about themselves and looking at the same from their friends to one where, "You have this constant stream of social approval indicators such as 'likes' and photo tags and comments and favorites and retweets coming at you in an app on your phone." This messed with users' brains in such a way that made it very difficult for them to *not* keep tapping the app. Once Facebook figured this out, of course, other social media platforms followed.[99]

Addiction to "social approval" is what these social media experiences caused. Needing to check and see if someone "likes" something posted creates the dopamine in the poster. Newport explains that we like to know that someone is thinking about us. This is what makes us constantly check these apps. Because of the addictive nature, people are spending more time on them than they realize, which takes them away from doing other activities. This behavior is causing people to feel unhappy or unfulfilled in their life and is ultimately contributing to health issues.

---

99 Newport, *Digital Minimalism: Choosing A Focused Life In A Noisy World*. 6–20

Driving one afternoon, I caught a radio interview with Newport on this topic. His voice was full of alarm as he explained that while the literature on this topic was still developing, it seems clear to most who are close to the research that there has been, "Major psychological harm, especially to adolescents who have had unrestricted access to social media mediated through smartphones." He went on to say it's looking like these behaviors causes sharp rises in anxiety and anxiety related disorders, corresponding hospitalizations for self-harm, and suicide attempts.

He said he hopes this issue gets enough attention so that by time his oldest child, who is six years old now, is old enough for a phone, the culture will have shifted so that the idea of giving his son or any twelve-year-old a smartphone would be considered outrageous. This cultural attitude shift that Newport is hoping for is, however, too late for iGen, who came of age with a smartphone in their hand.[100]

More Frequent Feedback

IGen's experience of seeking "social approval" constantly as teens may cause some of them to crave more frequent performance feedback from their managers than employees they managed previously.

Unlike millennials, this won't be because they think they should be promoted quickly—instead they'll be looking for reassurance that their job is secure.

---

[100] Newport, *Avoiding Digital Distraction*.

Many of these young adults will be anxious about their performance and want to know from you and others how they are doing. They have been socialized that "when they post something, everyone can weigh-in on it." So, when they do something, they will be waiting to see if you "like" it.

WHAT'S POSSIBLE

Having performance data does not always mean the data can be use consumed and understood easily. What's helping organizations gain insights are data visualization tools, also called Business Intelligence (BI). These tools connect a source of data to a dashboard that shows the information visually in graphs, charts, and tables. Tableau and Power BI are commonly used products in this regard.

iGen'er Will knows about data visualization. I interviewed Will as he was beginning his fourth week at his new job as an Associate Logistics Planner for an agricultural company of 10,000 employees, based in Minnesota. Having recently graduated with a degree in Supply Chain Management, Will was looking forward to learning as much as he could about his new company. He told me his team had recently started using Power BI. Since he had used the program during his last two summer internships, he was head winding the effort because no one else on his team had Power BI experience. He explained to me, "The background data is there. I build the visualizations we want to see. I can get the personal analytics, so I can filter down to see how many shipments someone has managed and how much money that's worth over a period of time."

Will has been looking forward to figuring out a way for his team to be able to summarize and filter performance data on demand using the Power BI. Having on demand performance feedback is something every iGen'er would value.

PERFORMANCE DATA – SUPPORT NEEDED

André Buckles, an HR executive was having trouble hiring sales underwriters for his company. He had on-average thirty-five to forty open positions, which was too many for this critical role.

He had a solution to propose. The solution required funding. He knew he needed data to make his case to fund the solution. He wanted a way to show the leaders that their company was not the only company struggling to hire sales underwriters in specific geographies, and that a new way of attracting this key talent was needed.

He wanted his company to use an Indeed job sponsorship tool. The tool would promote the sales underwriting jobs on Indeed's Industry specific career site and also put pop-up ad placements when individuals were searching for related jobs.

He had an agency look at the population of sales underwriters in the targeted areas, and look at what other companies were doing in terms of marketing and advertising for the positions in those areas.

Then they summarized this data on one PowerPoint slide. It was map of the United States that had bubbles showing available positions against available talent in several key cities. Plus, it showed how many other companies were also looking for this talent in those areas.

When Buckles presented the slide, it became clear to the leaders that they were not the only organization struggling to hire sales underwriters in those geographies.

"I displayed the data and I said, look, give me three months of (Indeed job) sponsorship. It's going to cost you 16,000 bucks we'll spread it across the geographies. And if we don't see any uptick, and we don't see it increasing the quality, and we're not able to get people, we'll stop."

The leaders agreed. The sponsorship tool was activated. Buckle's company did see uptick in the first six months "probably a 45 to 50% uptick in direct applicants to those roles." And they found that they were able to go from having around thirty-five to forty openings at any given time to more like twenty openings at any given time.

Data told the story that they needed a different recruiting tactic, and it also showed them the performance of those tactics.

Leaders,

Set a performance goal for yourself to develop a strategy to get performance data organized and digitally available on demand for each of your employees. Include in the scope to give them access to their previous years' data. Add AI[101] *smartness to it by showing them anonymized performance data of other individuals and groups to demonstrate what's possible and inspire them to achieve more.*

DO IT YOURSELF

If where you work doesn't have a formal method of providing performance feedback, design your own. One of my friends puts a reminder on her calendar each month to document her work accomplishments. This way when it is time for her to discuss her performance, she has notes ready to help her prepare. I have a folder in my work email where I put emails that were compliments, I received. (Sometimes, I will just look at these when I need a little encouragement!)

What I recommend is to schedule regular thirty-minute meetings with your manager. I suggest once a quarter, but not more frequent than monthly. Have this simple format: 1) Ask for feedback on how you are doing, 2) Provide your assessment on what's going well and what you are working on, and 3) Ask for advice.

Liz Ryan, a *Forbes* contributor, offers these additional suggestions:

☐ Don't be shy about asking for feedback or asking for advice on a situation you haven't handled before.

---

101 Artificial intelligence

☐ Don't forget to keep your manager informed of positive things you hear about the team, the company and your manager. Nobody gets enough acknowledgment!
☐ Don't assume your boss knows important news you hear or read during the day. If you think the new information would be valuable to your manager, pass it on.
☐ Don't assume that because your manager is different from you—in terms of gender, age, nationality or life story—that you can't be real with them. We can all bring more of ourselves to work, and it would be good for all of us if we did!

CHAPTER 9
PROFESSIONAL DEVELOPMENT DATA

One summer our neighborhood YMCA offered two-week intensive sessions for swimming instruction. They were limited to four children per instructor. I signed up our sons—Daniel and Chris.

Daniel, who was five years old, knew he couldn't swim. He was rightly concerned about drowning. Over our spring break, he had shown no interest in doing anything more than wading in the pool near the stairs.

On the other hand, Chris who was three had no idea he could not swim. On spring break, we had to be vigilant about making sure he had a life jacket or floaters on. No matter how closely we watched, he eventually would slip into the deeper end of the pool with his older cousins.

The first day of class we met the boys' swim instructor, Caesar. He was fit, friendly, and looked like he knew how to have fun with children. I explained to Caesar that my swim lesson goal for the summer was simple: I wanted each boy to be able to confidently jump into the deep end of the pool and swim to the side without drowning.

After the conversation Caesar's work began, and I had a poolside view.

The format each day was the same. Each class of four students lined up in front of the swim lane they were assigned. Caesar's lane was the one closest to the wall, where I sat. They did their warm-up outside of the pool. Afterwards, the kids either hung onto the side of the pool splashing each-other (Chris) or sat outside with their feet dangling in the water (Daniel). Then Caesar would demonstrate the swim drill they were to work on that day. One at a time, each child would do the drill with Caesar while the others watched.

Push me please

When it was Daniel's turn, he would obediently do the drill of the day, but his fear while doing it was palpable. As he paddled along, Caesar was by his side in the water the whole way. Daniel would whimper in fear as he progressed down the swim lane. But he never gave up. He finished the drill every time.

Daniel's journey down the swim lane was painful for me to witness. I hated that he was uncomfortable while doing the drill.

Yet when he made it to the end of lane, he got out of the pool and strutted past me back to the beginning of their swim lane. I saw the confidence that only comes from overcoming your fear sweep over him. It was beautiful.

Don't stop me

When it was Chris's turn, he would shoot off the side of the pool and submerge his head. After what seemed like an eternity his head would pop up a couple of yards farther in the lane, and he'd squirt the water out of his mouth. Caesar kept by Chris's side as he propelled along. He would paddle forward furiously and again he'd submerge under the water for what seemed like a few seconds. Then his head would pop up a yard farther down the lane. This continued until he got to the end of the lane. There, he would pop out of the pool. Then he'd skip back to the front of the swim lane, giving me a huge smile as passed by me. The moment was pure joy.

Caesar could tell Daniel and Chris approached the swim lessons differently. He provided them the specific support they each needed, and it worked. They worked hard and proudly mastered swimming that summer, thanks to Caesar.

PROFESSIONAL DEVELOPMENT DATA

In the workplace, professional development data is generated in numerous ways—it can be an annual event or more frequent. It is a measure of what an employee is personally working on to grow professionally. Often, it takes the form of a plan with goals to be achieved over a specified period.

This is done in partnership with the manager of the employee. It is meant to both **push an employee to grow** (e.g. develop more skills through new experiences or instruction) and **support an employee who is ready for the next challenge** (e.g. new jobs or projects).

Professional development data is the information collected related to an employee's professional growth.[102]

Like Chris and Daniel, I have had some good instructors over years, and some good managers that pushed me and cheered me on. When I was in banking, we had a steadfast professional development protocol that we followed. Each year, we set professional development goals, documented them, and shared them with our managers. Each quarter, we sat down and reviewed our progress towards these goals with our manager. The Human Resources representative, Brenda, was assigned to ensure our managers did this. She kept track. If someone hadn't met with their team members on time, their name appeared on the list of those out of compliance. The situation would usually be quickly resolved.

---

102 Some companies encourage employees to include goals from their personal life too in their plans. (e.g. run a marathon, better work-life balance, learn a new language).

I looked forward to those coaching meetings. I wanted to advance in my career and was willing to work hard but didn't necessarily know what I needed to do. I didn't know how it worked. Getting the guidance and feedback quarterly was something that really helped me have conversations about professional growth. Some of the advice still echoes in my mind today. I had a manager, Bob Greco, who has especially encouraging. One time when I had tried something new and it didn't result in exactly what I'd hoped, he said to me, "If you aren't making some mistakes, you aren't pushing yourself enough."

This was good advice for me to keep in mind when setting my goals. Goals should be hard and a little scary. When you have a supportive manager like Bob, you are more likely to push yourself.

The act of having goals helps us focus on the right behaviors and steers us away from those that don't serve us. There's also research that says the having a coach (or manager or mentor) makes a difference.[103]

DEVELOPING RELATIONAL EQUITY

Laura Seredinski, the HR leader we met in Chapter 2, says employees should push themselves to build "relational equity." To me this means is make it a goal to invest time getting to know colleagues at work.

To facilitate relational equity development, Seredinski

---

[103] Doyle, *Does Coaching Work? New Scientific Evidence Points to Yes.*

is tactical about creating opportunities for connection to occur in the workplace community. She works with leaders to create events for employees to meet such as employee run seminars on items of personal interest like 'flying drones' or 'mindfulness.' She's also had success with team-sponsored social events especially when she has had teams compete to see whose events are most well-attended.

Seredinski explains the social interactions at the events build relationships and binds people to the organization, which increases retention and professional development.

"When employees have strong relationships, they also will have a strong network and with that, they start to find their own path." Seredinski explains that organizations like hers that are "growing and scaling will have a lot of room for people to grow professionally" but they need to put themselves out there by building relationships.

Many employees would rather have their career journey scripted for them. Seredinski says, "The number one thing I have been hearing in my focus groups with people (employees) is that they really want a designed career path or career growth journey. I don't want to dismiss that. But, I'm just saying, we're a pretty flat organization. So, it's unlikely to happen. Employees need to connect to each other to learn about internal opportunities and establish their relational equity."

She explains, "When you have relational equity with the right people, they work with you to find a role that works for you, but within the organizational structure that continues to add value to the company."

PROFESSIONAL DEVELOPMENT—YOUNG ADULTS

Several of my peers have shared with me that the millennials they have managed have been looking for fast professional development and advancement.[104] A survey conducted by the software firm Qualtrics and venture capital firm Accel Partners, found that of the 1,500 millennials surveyed, roughly eighty percent said that "an emphasis on personal growth is the most important quality of a company's culture." They value training and see training that offers a blended approach where they can access online content and offline coaching is ideal.[105]

iGen'ers are different than millennials. Jean Twenge, generational researcher, explains iGen'ers won't expect to be CEO of the company within five years. They will be eager to do a good job but will be afraid of making mistakes. This means most likely you are going to need to push them to develop. Provide them regular and directed guidance, carefully spell out what skills they need to master and experiences they need to have in order to continue to develop as you know they can.

---

104 Millennials were born 1981- 1996.
105 Jenkins. "This Is The No. 1 Thing Millennials Consider When Starting A Job."

WHAT'S POSSIBLE

Knowing your professional development plan and having access to it in whatever form it takes, not only from the current year but past years, is extremely valuable. The professional development data could be from a formal development process (e.g. results of a professional growth goal setting questionnaire) or notes from coaching sessions with a manager.

Being able to see the changes from year to year allows an employee to see their story of growth.

- Knowing what they have made progress on will reinforce their hard work.
- Conversely, if they see that progress has not been made or they have slipped backward, they will be likely to understand that what they are doing isn't working.

iGen'er Molly is in a two-year management training program with a large beer brewing company. She's able to see her development plan clearly because her company has laid it out for her. When I asked her about it, she explained that when you go into entry level sales, you have to pay your dues—and that's all right with her.

"There are a lot of small things I've got to do that kind of seem menial, but I need to do them now because I'm still very much learning. I really appreciate getting to do this type of learning in an industry with a product that I believe in and like. Also, it's a topic (her industry) that people are interested in, which makes it more enjoyable for me, as I go through this learning period, as I'm starting my career," she says.

Molly is looking forward to gaining knowledge and skills in her program. Having concise expectations of skills she needs to develop, and experiences she needs to have works well for her.

Leaders,

Assess how your organization is supporting your employees' professional development. Develop a strategy for not only ensuring your employees are encouraged to work on their professional growth, but also for establishing how their development information can be readily accessible to them, in a way that can ignite in them their desire to grow and develop along with your organization. When you demonstrate that professional growth matters, you also send the message that your employees matter and are wanted on your journey.

DO IT YOURSELF

If you don't have a manager or coach to insist you set development goals, set your own goals and share them with one or more trusted friends. Scott Garber, founder of the Young Entrepreneur Council (YEC), does this as do many of his fellow YEC members.

"Every year a friend and I get out of New York City and spend an entire weekend writing out our goals for the next ten years, five years, and one year in a shared folder in Google Drive. We break the one-year goals down into quarterly, monthly, weekly and daily goals. Each Tuesday at 7 a.m., we hop on a call to share news of where we are and to hold one another accountable. It's been huge," says Garber.

Garber assembled a list from some of his Young Entrepreneur Council (YEC) members of their favorite tools to capture and monitor both personal growth and work goals. They ranged from using a white board and giant post-it notes to apps like Way of Life, Any.do, Wunderlist, Clear, and Google Tasks.

Pick a method to capture your goals and document them. Then the next most important step is to share them with a person or two that you trust.[106]

---

106 Gerber. "11 Best Tools For Setting And Tracking Goals."

CHAPTER 10
OPERATIONS DATA

After many years doing big data analytics projects in Human Capital Management, Dr. Wendy Lynch is now also speaking on and conducting workshops on a topic that has become her passion: "clear and meaningful conversations that promote mutual understanding and success." Her recent book, *Get to What Matters*, lays out her techniques for how to transform conversations at work. Many people who are masterful at conversations have honed their skills by experiencing others who have these soft skills. That was the case with Wendy, who learned by observing her co-author and colleague Clydette de Groot. Together they teamed up and created this book for others, who have not had the good fortune of having a role model.

Get to What Matters talks about the importance of having and remembering "the intention" of conversations at work. Keeping in mind the intention can be your rudder when the conversation meanders around, which it often does when people come together to work through something important to them.[107]

OPERATIONS RELATED TO PRODUCTS AND SERVICES

Many businesses' operations have the intention to generate data. Some of the data is needed in order for the next step in the business process to happen. Additionally, other data created is simply a by-product of the operation's business process.

> **Operations data is generated from an organization's operations and business processes.**

Think of a package delivery company. When someone drops off a package to be delivered at their local UPS store, the information about the package is captured electronically. Then the package is sorted and grouped with other packages that will eventually end up in a truck, to be delivered to the addressee's door. The driver of that truck—let's say his name is Doug—needs the list of stops, the corresponding packages to deliver, and a suggested route. Doug will get this essential information electronically. It may be on a handheld device or a screen in his truck.

---

107 *Get2whatmatters.Com*

Donncha Carroll and Axiom Partners provide deep analytics and decision support expertise to large companies around the world. Carroll understands how companies are using operational data today. He explains that operations create data that shows what happened as a result of a business process.

Carrol told me the term for this data is "digital exhaust," which literally made me laugh out loud. I told him that I thought I was going to need a mask! He agreed it was an odd term.

In the UPS example, when Doug is done with his shift, there will be digital information that tells the story of what happened. It will include data about which packages Doug delivered on time, and which ones were late.

What if the digital exhaust was shared routinely with Doug in a way that he could interact with and study? My guess is that Doug would generate some ideas for how to improve his processes. For example, he may suggest a different route the next time this combination of stops is needed, since he has experienced the terrain in-person.

OPERATIONS RELATED TO EMPLOYEES
In addition to operations that are related to a company's products or services, companies have operations that are related solely to their employees. The resulting business processes also generate data that are tied to the person.

This information could include:[108]

- Employee online activity on a work computer/system such as browsing history, search history, and information regarding the employee's interaction with an Internet Web site, application, or advertisement.
- Employee badge activity that shows where and when a badge was swiped.
- Audio and video conferencing data.
- New hire/onboarding paperwork, including resumés, employee applications, background checks, and tax forms.
- Payroll information, including employee bank account numbers for direct deposit.
- Credit card information provided in connection with expense reports.
- Random drug testing paperwork and results.
- Documenting of various types of leave, such as sick leave, vacation, and paid time off.
- Employee benefit plans.
- Employee exit surveys.

WHAT'S POSSIBLE

Dr. Lynch explained to me that by combining data sources, scientists can get business insights like predictive capabilities that can result in better intervention. They can identify places to insert AI[109] into operations like prompts. In the

---

108 "Theodore Augustinos, Laura Ferguson, Ben Frazzini Kendrick, Emily Holpert, Sean Kilian, Ricardo Lopez, Glenn Pudelka, Molly McGinnis Stine, Elizabeth Tosaris, Locke Lord LLP. Jdsupra.com , August 20, 2019.
109 Artificial intelligence

UPS example, if Doug has put on more miles than expected during a shift, a message to drop the truck off for servicing at the end of the shift could be sent to him. Here is a story that illustrates the results of combining data sources.

IMPROVING QUALITY OF CARE[110]

By combining people data sources—including health care, compensation, attendance, performance, prevention, safety and risk management—a large utility was able to determine which sub-groups of employees to focus on in order to make the biggest impact. The utility's employees hold a variety of roles, from handling service calls to climbing utility poles. Their team of data scientists recommended the two key subgroups of employees to focus on: 1) the top five percent of healthcare/benefit users, and 2) linemen.

The top 5 percent of healthcare/benefit users

The analysis showed that 1,000 employees (five percent of base) drove forty-eight percent of total benefit costs at $55,700 per person per year. Additionally, this group averaged seventy-three lost days per person per year, compared to forty-four days for others. The company offered this group extra services. They contracted to have intervention support provided. The staff reached out over the telephone to the 1,000 employees targeted. Of those reached, eighty-five percent chose to enroll. Now, the utility has expanded the offer of support from five percent to twenty percent of employees. The data

---

110 Sprangler,"Workplace Mental Health - Pacific Gas & Electric.".

showed that a good portion of the employees in the top five percent of healthcare/benefit users' group were in the top twenty percent group the year earlier. By offering the custom support earlier to the approximately 4,000 employees, the goal is to increase chances the employees can get back on track with complex health management before their situation gets worse.

Linemen

The data showed that as a group the Linemen—the people who climb the utility poles—had a higher incidence of tobacco-related cancer, compared to the rest of the company's physical workforce. The need to focus on this employee group was further confirmed when the team factored in the company's training investment in these employees and their job's high-risk tasks. In addition to addressing tobacco usage by increasing awareness and encouraging use of the free tobacco cessation programs, the solution for the lineman group included addressing their lifestyle choices.

To do this, the team added a full-day class to the pre-apprentice lineman-training curriculum. It focused on fitness and nutrition strategies that reduce the risk of cumulative wear and tear on your body. The message was clear: linemen can enjoy a twenty-year career without having to endure physical agony if they adopt a healthy lifestyle. Plans were made to develop similar classes for more tenured linemen.

IDENTIFYING KEY INFLUENCERS

Carroll provided me an example of how his firm helped an insurance company that was making a large-scale change by using email data to understand who the company's key influencers were. They looked at who sent emails to whom. From this they could identify the people that were connecting key groups of individuals. Then, they leveraged this insight in their change management strategy.

"We made sure that we brought those folks on board, brought them into a series of conversations, shared the change knowing that those folks were going to be instrumental in making the change happen," says Carroll.

Additionally, once the change was announced over email, Carroll's firm monitored the subject line of emails to understand "who was talking about a particular topic." They were able to advise the insurance company on additional communications needed (e.g. what were people concerned about? What were they not understanding?) by studying the email data.

Leaders,

Establish (or review your current) inventory of operational data that contains people data. Understand what you have. Bring leaders together to consider how this information could be used to improve your business if it was integrated and available to use toward gaining insights.

- ☐ *Consider a problem you have, where a solution has been proposed but you are hesitating to implement it because you don't have a solid way to measure if it worked.*
- ☐ *Consider a safety issue that keeps you up at night—you would like to be able to detect it early, before it gets out of control.*
- ☐ *Consider a question the public or employees are asking you, that would be better answered with factual data.*

Then, decide what you will go after first. Select a leader to form a small team to make it happen. Additionally, be sure to let the team know as they learn more about the value of using people data, you look forward to them sharing what they have learned with you and your team.

PART THREE

CHAPTER 11

USING PEOPLE DATA

Occasionally, it hits me: there was a time before the Internet, and I was alive then. Somehow, I managed to do things that today I would totally rely on my smartphone to help me with.

In August 2019, my family navigated our way around New York City in a rented van that was loaded with our sons' college stuff. Stop one was the Bronx, for Chris. Stop two was Washington D.C., for Daniel.

While in the Bronx, we ended up driving from the hotel there over to Manhattan for dinner with my Uncle Bob and Aunt Michelle. The next day we drove from the hotel to Fordham at the Rose Hill campus where we unloaded half of the van's contents. Then we drove Chris's hockey bag to the ice rink that was somewhere else—all while relying on the Maps app on our smartphones to get us around the curvy highways. We wove in and out of lanes, moving and not moving with hundreds of other cars. Because traffic is a huge variable in New York City, the routes suggested by our app never seemed to be the same. We really did not get the lay of the land on that trip. We were grateful for the directions and all the other information—like where to get gas—that were provided to us on our app, and not really sure how we would have managed without it.

As my husband John and I reflected on the adventure, we reminisced about how we used to do it before smartphones. I recalled the AAA Trip Tix from my youth. My mom would call the AAA branch and tell them where we were going. She would then go pick it up. When she brought it home, I was excited to look it over in anticipation of our trip. I loved looking at maps then, and I still do today.

The AAA agents would draw the route with a highlighter on a series of pages of numbered maps. They would then stack them up in order. Then spiral bind them together. The result was a small book about twice the size of my smartphone.

As you traveled the route and as the trip progressed, you would turn the page. We had the Trip Tix with us in our family van as we traveled from Appleton Wisconsin to Sarasota, Florida for Spring break. I remember being encouraged each time when "the page was turned"–this meant we were getting closer to the beach.

However, I like my Maps app a hundred percent more than the Trip Tix. My Maps app talks to me. It re-routes me when necessary. It is really good at estimating how long it'll take to get somewhere. My Maps app is a great travel companion.

SECOND TIME IS THE CHARM

A month later, for Fordham's parents' weekend, John and I flew into LaGuardia and rented a car. While we still relied on our smartphones to guide us, we also recognized some of the names of the bridges and streets and other landmarks. It felt more comfortable.

I think working with new data can be like this—especially combined datasets that I haven't used before. At first it is unfamiliar. The data field names are not always obvious. How they are presented doesn't always tell a story I understand. I have to ask a lot of questions. I have to look at it a few different ways. I do find though—after I've seen it a few times and worked with it—that I understand it. I can recognize "the particular curves" and know what they mean.

Leaders,

In the previous section I shared with you the types of people data typically created and available to you. In this section, I will illustrate how others are repurposing this data and using it for other business reasons, like detecting and solving problems and answering questions.

As you read through these chapters, consider how you can use people data to augment what you are already doing to make you and your leaders more effective with managing people.

CHAPTER 12

DETECT PROBLEMS. PROMOTE SAFETY

In 1990, the vogue leadership style was a top-down approach. It was all about getting employees motivated to work harder through fear and force. Leaders like Jack Walsh from General Electric sought to motivate their employees by proclaiming ten percent of their workforce would be fired every year.

This same year, Dr. William A. Kahn from Boston University published research about a type of leadership style that clashed loudly with the in-fashion "gain ground no matter the cost" approach.

Kahn coined this new style "engagement." He explained that engagement in reference to employees and their workplace is fundamentally about "how your employees feel about work."

Kahn argued that employees will give more to their jobs if they are engaged. This means they feel that:

- They are doing something important to contribute to organizational success.
- They have rewarding and supportive relationships with supervisors and coworkers.
- They are afforded the physical and psychological resources they needed to accomplish their work.

This research resonated with many in the human resource and organizational behavior scene. Before too long, there were many firms providing the service to design surveys that would measure engagement for companies.

These surveys help leaders uncover where there were problems with manager-employee relationships or business processes that resulted in employees making choices to not bring themselves fully into their work.[111]

PAPER SURVEYS

Back in 1995, I was working at a regional bank, First Chicago. After an announcement was made that First Chicago was merging with another regional bank, NBD, I was moved to a role on the "Transition" team.

---

111 Reem, "William Kahn: Father Of Employee Engagement."

Along with a dozen others at First Chicago, we worked with a similar sized group from NBD. Our charge was to facilitate teams of leaders doing the work to set up the integration of the two companies. These teams were responsible for determining what the new organization should look like—which leaders should lead certain groups, which technology applications should be used, which technology applications should be sunset, which bank branches should stay open, and which ones should be closed.

It was hard, emotionally-charged work because, of course, some people were going to lose their jobs and others would end up with jobs that they perceived as a step down from what they had before the merger.

During this time, we received an employee engagement survey.

When the survey was distributed, it was on paper. The paper surveys had a set of questions with multiple choice answers and a few open-ended write-in questions. Our team was responsible for analyzing the results and providing a summary to leadership.

The surveys were scanned, and the results of the multiple choice questions were tabulated by a computer.

At that point in time, there was no technology that could accurately read the handwritten answers to the open-ended questions. The decision was made that these handwritten survey answers would be sampled. I don't remember how many surveys were completed, but I do know there were 35,000 employees between the two organizations.

One of my colleagues was distraught by the idea of someone's handwritten answers not being looked at. She made the case that every one of the handwritten answers should be reviewed and offered to do it herself. I remember her sitting at her desk for days with a huge stack of paper surveys on her desk. Eventually, she finished the task and provided a good summary for our team to analyze.

Since then, technology has evolved. Today most surveys are completed digitally, and you can type in your comments. These typed comments can be easily scanned and sorted by content type and served up for analysis. For example, one set could get all the comments that have the words "manager" or "management" in them, another set could be all the comments that have the words "weekends" or "trust" or "good."

Today, digital communication like your emails and instant messages can be scanned by technology and flagged. This is done passively. That means you don't have to do anything.

RED LIGHTS

Some people think that an employer shouldn't collect their employees' behavioral data passively. They see this as a violation of privacy. When I told a few people about my topic and explained that people data collection was typical in workplaces, some were creeped out.

These were generally people who have not worked in a corporate setting lately. They seemed quite unsettled to learn that behavioral data and digital activity, such as emails and browsing history, may also be collected by employers in many corporations.

I was surprised at the intensity of the reaction by some as they tossed the "big brother" phrase at me. Perhaps I've become desensitized to the phenomena, since at one point in my career I was reminded daily when I logged into my work computer that my email could be read.

Or maybe it's because in Chicago, where I live, our household has received multiple red-light tickets mailed to our home with an invitation to *watch the video* of proof that indeed someone drove our car through a red light.

As disheartening and expensive as those red light tickets were, they did "detect the problem" of someone going through a red light, or driving too fast through a school zone.

When we would receive a ticket, we would study it and discuss where it happened, who was likely driving, and how we needed to "watch it" in that area and "drive more safely."

CHECK ENGINE
Your dreaded check-engine light has come on. You know that when this happens you need to stop and look under the hood to find out what's going on with your car.

There was no check-engine light for Enron's board of directors when Andrew Fastow was their Chief Financial Officer. If there had been, would the Enron collapse have been stopped before their 21,000 employees were encouraged to move their retirement money into Enron stock that later became worthless?

Data scientists at KeenCorp think so.

Enron was the American energy, commodities, and services company that became infamous when it fell fast and hard into bankruptcy in 2001. Fastow, the thirty-seven-year-old fast-rising star had figured out how to please Enron founder, Kenneth Lay, by keeping the stock price high with financial tricks that fooled the market.

Ten years after Enron's collapse, KeenCorp was founded. KeenCorp and companies like them provide special software that produce a Key Performance Indicator (KPI) for leaders about their employees' engagement. If employees are engaged, the KPI is high. If they are disengaged, the KPI is low.

KeenCorp's special software does what's called sentiment analysis. It's not reading emails per se, but rather scanning them for word patterns and their context. It does a calculation that results in a KPI that in turn lets a leader know if there's a risk that needs exploring. This is done with unstructured data, like the comments field in a survey question.[112]

---

112 Gupta, "Sentiment Analysis: Concept, Analysis and Applications."

Data scientists at KeenCorp analyzed several years' worth of emails sent by Enron's top 150 executives. The analysis seemed to check out with key moments in the company's collapse except for one date: June 28, 1999. According to their software's algorithm, email sentiment showed tensions were high that day, but the scientists were not able to find record of any public event on that specific date.

They tracked down Fastow in Amsterdam after one of his speaking engagements on Ethics. Fastow confirmed there was an internal event on June 28, 1999. The company's Board of Directors had spent hours discussing a proposal Fastow made known as "LJM" which involved dubious transactions that would bolster Enron's financial statements and eventually lead to their collapse. According to Fastow, no one said, "This is wrong; we shouldn't do it."

However, according the KeenCorp analysis, the executives' emails were showing sentiments of stress. If the June 28, 1999 emails had been scanned that week, those monitoring the health of the company would have seen the "check engine" warning light shining bright red.[113]

---

113 Elkin. "The Confessions of Andy Fastow."

CIAO BELLA

When I was in college, my friend Annabelle and I spent a semester in Southern France. We were only a two-hour train ride from Italy, so we often went there for the weekends. We loved the Italian countryside, the food, and the friendly people.

Turns out they liked us too. Being two blonde twenty-one-year-old American women, we often found young Italian men willing to show us their city's sights.

On one occasion, our guides—Sergio and Alonzo—got into a heated argument with each other. They were passionately conversing in Italian. Neither Annabelle nor I spoke Italian. Annabelle seemed worried about their conversation; I wasn't. While I didn't know Italian, I could sense what they were talking about from their tones and gestures. Plus, I picked up a word here or there that sounded like the English equivalent, for example *ristorante* or *motociclo*.

So, I started telling Annabelle in English what I thought they were saying, to reassure her. I told her that they were arguing over which restaurant we should go to, and whether or not they should take us on their motorcycles.

My "translating" got Sergio's attention, he stopped arguing with Alonzo and bellowed at me "You know Italian!" To which I replied, "Close enough!"

That's what data scientists like Ben Waber PhD, do with voice data that they collect for organizations. Waber says analyzing voice data is like you are "watching a foreign film, but have turned off the subtitles so you don't know what people are saying but you get the sense that this guy likes this guy or these people are having a heated discussion."[114]

WEARABLES

When Waber was a student working on his PhD, he worked in the Media Lab at MIT. There, he and his team were working on "wearables." Wearables are devices containing technology that can be worn.

The wearables he was working on were badges not unlike what many people use today to swipe in and out of their large office buildings. Like these, Waber's badges were tied to an individual but also captured their voice and location data.

The badges were being used to "better understand salary negotiations—how much money you might actually make based on your tone of voice, how much you interrupt

---

114 Waber, "Creating Better Organizations Based On How Its Members Interact."

someone...these badges collected data on how people talked to each other—not content, it was who talks to whom, location, and movement data."

They also used the badges to capture voice data to test if voice data could be analyzed to predict how productive and happy people were. They learned that the voice data collected from the wearable badges were found to be "'six times more predictive" of productivity and happiness than survey or email data.

Inspired by these results, Waber and his partners did more research to further advance voice analysis technology. They wondered if you could directly tie tone of voice to stress levels.

To do this research, they involved hundreds of people. They provided badges to be worn at work and dozens of time-stamped vials for participants to spit into every fifteen minutes. The vials were collected and the spit in them was analyzed for cortisone levels. Cortisone is the main hormone released by the adrenal gland in response to stress. The spit data was compared to the voice data with the same time stamp.

The test proved that voice data could be used to predict "how stressed out people were in real time by looking at a change in the tone of voice."

This means if a company has thousands of these devices in several locations, they can know in about two hours where the most stressed group is in the company and investigate to learn what's going on.[115]

BEHAVIORAL DATA VERSUS EMPLOYEE FEEDBACK

In addition to privacy concerns, others who work with leaders on improving employee engagement caution against relying solely on passive data to indicate cultural health or employee wellbeing.

Laura Hamill through the firm she co-founded, Limeade, works with their customers to translate engagement survey data into actionable strategies and hands-on workshops to better employee engagement.

When it comes to the analysis of email or voice data to detect problems, Hamill expressed the importance of keeping direct feedback from employees at the forefront of workplace analysis.

"We need to embrace how people feel about work. It is not only a legitimate thing to measure, but it is the most important thing to measure. And I think a lot of people are starting to come along to that, and they're starting to see that it is what matters."

Hamill cautions there are plenty of naysayers out there who may want to measure other items that are flat-out easier to count than an employee's level of engagement. She says these items are less relevant and measuring them causes an

---

[115] Ibid.

organization "to continue in a cycle of focusing on things that don't matter and don't fundamentally improve our work or the results we achieve."

One without the other, isn't enough especially in a large organization with multiple locations and many people working remotely. A monitoring strategy should include analysis of active data like (e.g. engagement surveys) and passive data (e.g. email or voice data).

Leaders,

By analyzing data, you can detect problems which you can then, of course, address. Employee engagement surveys can shine a light on what needs to be addressed. The city of Chicago had cameras that identified my family's need to "watch-it" when we drive. Programs that scan email data and voice data can pick up on tensions brewing in your company.

When you are responsible for the safety of employees spread across geographies with some only engaging online with each other, having ways to detect problems as they are happening makes sense.

Leverage the data you have and, as you do, be transparent with everyone about it. Tell them what data you are collecting and how you are going to use it.

Frequent engagement data can let you know how well you are doing at creating and sustaining the culture you need.

Done right, monitoring will put people at ease. We do a significant amount of work online. Scanning digital data is the equivalent to you listening in the elevator or in the lunch line. Use the data you have and keep your employees safe.

CHAPTER 13

ANSWER QUESTIONS. REAFFIRM.

In 2015, Salesforce, a software company, pulled the compensation data of their 30,000 employees together. At a conference in December 2018, Salesforce Chief Personnel Officer Cindy Robbins told the story of why the compensation data had been compiled.[116]

Robbins and others at Salesforce felt strongly that a pay gap existed at their company. In 2015, she came to the realization that it was time for Salesforce to address equal pay differently. In addition to softer initiatives that the leadership had been supporting—like mentoring and speakers—Robbins wanted

---

116 Stahl. "Leading By Example To Close The Gender Pay Gap."

compensation discrepancies directly addressed. To do this, she knew she needed hard data.[117]

While analyses of Census Bureau data was available that indicated that women working full time on average made eighty cents compared to every dollar men make, Robbins wanted her company's data. She wanted Salesforce data.[118]

What she really wanted was a compensation audit.

When Robbins approached Salesforce CEO Marc Benioff with the compensation audit request, he was taken aback and perhaps he was a little offended too.[119] In a *60 Minutes* interview with Lesley Stahl, Benioff recalls that he didn't believe there was a pay gap problem. He thought Salesforce was doing a lot to make sure there was equal opportunity. However, he agreed to audit.

The audit analyzed the compensation of Salesforces' 30,000 employees, and the results shocked Benioff. He told Lesley Stahl emphatically that, "It (the pay gap) was just everywhere. It was through the whole company, every division, every department, every geography." Yes, he was surprised, really surprised because "Salesforce has clear policies that men and women should be paid equally."[120]

---

117   Ibid.
118   Ibid.
119   Bastone, "Salesforce's Chief People Officer Explains How And Why The Company Has Spent $8.7 Million To Close Its Gender Pay Gap."
120   Stahl, "Leading By Example To Close The Gender Pay Gap"

To his credit, Benioff addressed the gaps with three million dollars in compensation adjustments in 2016 that resulted in a pay increase for six percent of their workforce.

REAFFIRMING

Benioff had the audit repeated in 2017 and again in 2018. After which Benioff agreed to invest $3 million and $2.7 million respectively to address the gaps in each year.

Why the need to adjust three years in row? Robbins explained that in 2017 Salesforce had acquired fourteen companies and that "when you acquire fourteen companies, you acquire not just their technology and their people, but also their pay practices."

Robbins went on to explain that, as long as pay equity is a priority for Salesforce, an audit would be needed every year. She says, "That's one thing I aligned with Marc on very early on, that this was not a one and done thing."

Robbins is quick to say, "The power is in the data. Every company, no matter the size of your company, you have all the data. There's really no excuse not to look at it." [121]

TRANSPARENCY

Another company dealing in all kinds of data is TransUnion (TU), a global information and insights company. Their

---

121 Bastone, "Salesforce's Chief People Officer Explains How And Why The Company Has Spent $8.7 Million To Close Its Gender Pay Gap."

website says, "We're a sophisticated, global risk information provider striving to use information for good."

In my interview with Katie Coleman, a human resources executive at TU, the topic of transparency came up immediately. Coleman explained to me that there's so much data on the public site Glassdoor that TU employees, past and present, have put out there.

Glassdoor is a job site that, in addition to having job listings, has information provided by employees about their own companies. Current and past employees post company reviews, they rate the CEO, and provide salary information.

Coleman said when it comes to TU information on Glassdoor, "Thousands and thousands of employees have self-reported their salary information." When I asked her if they were giving accurate information. She said they were. She would know—among other things, she's responsible for tracking compensation.

Because of the public presence of salary information, Coleman feels if you're not providing that data internally, you should be. It helps you manage the pressure that's coming your way soon—if you aren't feeling it already. Pressure like, what should a manager say when an employee walks up to them and says, "Hey, I was on Glassdoor and I saw that everyone here that works as a consultant makes twenty grand more than I do. Where's my money?"

Coleman is quick to say that's not an easy conversation for anyone to have.

At TU, compensation information is shared. "We still keep individual salary information confidential but share much more about our practices and market data," says Coleman. They have had lots of conversations about financial transparency. As part of their annual compensation process, they share salary ranges and share sources for the market data they used.

Additionally, they are focusing on education for their managers. They want their managers ready for those conversations. They want them to understand the compensation data and be able to make sense of it, so they can have meaningful conversations about it with their employees.

Leaders,

By analyzing data, you can answer questions. Whether it's a nagging feeling that your overall compensation is not as fair as advertised, or it's an employee questioning if their compensation is fair—analyzing data sets the record straight.

Taking the time to organize your people data allows you to answer questions with confidence and authority. Plus, you can use the information as foundational facts when looking at changes to implement, like modifying compensation the way Salesforce did versus relying on incomplete information.

When you answer questions about management practices— especially those related to fairness—with facts, you have better conversations. Plus, coupling access to good data with education on how to use the data improves the quality of decisions.

CHAPTER 14

TEST SOLUTIONS. SOLVE PROBLEMS

Cate Kinder, a Chicago human resources generalist, often found herself creating order by establishing systems to help HR operations run more smoothly.

Her employer collected lots of employee data: demographics, employee benefits information, payroll data, performance review results, and more (like what seminars employees attended and what training they took).

Kinder says, "We didn't really do anything with it other than check the boxes. The question was always 'Is this done (collected)?' Yes or no. Then the data would just sit there."

Often Kinder would find herself engaged in conversation with the firm's partners about how to get their "numbers" people to be more successful as people managers. They were accountants after all, so dealing with people wasn't their strong suit.

Kinder recalls a partner at her firm bringing one of his managers, Marco, to her attention. Marco worked at an office in the western suburbs of Chicago.[122]

The partner said he was hearing that Marco's team members had been voicing concerns that Marco had become so tightly wound that, without warning, he would just snap at people. The result was a hostile workplace environment.

Kinder was concerned about this information. She knew Marco "to be the nicest guy in the world" and wondered what was going on. She asked the partner if he had any idea about what was going on. He said that Marco just needed some help from HR to be a better manager.

Kinder did some digging. She knew the offices had information that showed how many audit reports were being produced by each area, each month. She investigated what was going on in Marco's office. She saw that a significant spike in the volume of reports in Marco's area had occurred at the close of the previous quarter. She knew the size of his team and was shocked to see that they had produced as much as they had. She wondered, "How on earth have they had gotten this much work done?"

---

[122] Name changed to protect privacy.

Kinder shared her finding with the partner who had voiced the concern about Marco. He too was surprised. He did his own digging and learned that another office had dumped the work onto Marco's team without advance warning. He also learned that Marco had not asked for extra resources to support the additional work. Kinder coached the partner on how to sit down with Marco and talk about how the firm appreciated Marco's gallant efforts, yet needed him to assess situations like this in the future and ask for support to ensure the stress-level for him and his team would be kept in check.

QUALITATIVE DATA

People who manage others are the connective tissues of an organization. Their jobs have lots of variables—namely their team members. Often, they run into challenges and could use some extra support. When feedback is provided, those who are standing by to offer support have what they need to further investigate the situation.

Qualitative information, like the team members' feedback that the partner at Kinder's firm passed onto her, is data. Like any data, it has value and should not be discarded. With advances in technology, today leaders can not only get employee data directly from conversations with employees, they can also collect it fairly quickly from surveys and behavioral data.

BEHAVIORAL DATA

Behavioral data is information produced as a result of actions.

In speaking with data scientists, I found it interesting that some had strong opinions about which data was more valuable: qualitative or behavioral.

There's a camp of scientists who, while thinking qualitative data like Kinder's employee feedback or the survey has its place, nevertheless prefer behavioral data. Ben Waber, PhD is one of those scientists.

Waber is recognized worldwide as an expert in people analytics, collaboration, and wearable technology. His LinkedIn profile says that he is, "Particularly passionate about the power of behavioral data and analytics to improve organizations and how people work in general."

I was fascinated by the way Waber and his teams use behavior data to solve organizational problems. In one of his videos, he provides an example of a network of bank branches that were analyzed for a large bank. While the branches were incentivized to meet team loan goals, some branches were significantly underperforming.[123]

The employees at all the bank branches were given badges to wear that produced information about each individual's movement. Waber's team explored the badge data to understand if there were any patterns.

They looked at who was talking to whom, their location, and movement data. They found some patterns.

---

[123] "Mapping Employee Chitchat Can Reveal Information Blockages."

The branches fell into three groups. The first group were the higher performing branches. In all these branches, the interactions were balanced between team members.

The second group was a set of under-performing branches. Here they noticed that these branches always had two subgroups of team members that were communicating within their group, but not with other groups.

The third group were branches that had one, two or three outliers that were mainly communicating with one person, not with others in the branch. The outliers were not seeming to mix at all with the rest of the branch employees.

To learn what would cause a branch to fall into one of the three groups, Waber and his team went on field trips to the branches. After some observations and interviews with branch members, they found the answers.

The first group of branches, the higher performing branches, were located in buildings that only had one floor. All the employees worked on the same floor. Employees here talked with everyone.

The second group of branches, the underperforming ones, were located in buildings that had employees on two floors. What happened here was the employees tended to mainly only converse with those who worked on their own floor. Waber and his team theorized that because of this, they were missing on out on intelligence that they could gain from those on the other floor.

The third group, the one with outliers, had everyone on the same floor as group one, so that wasn't a factor. What they learned was the outliers were new employees who had been with the bank over a month but were still only interacting with their direct managers.[124]

TESTING RECOMMENDED SOLUTIONS
Waber gets excited when he talks about behavioral data's ability to solve problems. Being a true scientist, he uses data to test theories. He is a strong advocate for companies testing new management practices before rolling them out. He further explains that a solution that works for one company may not work for another. Often, there are too many differences between companies, culture being one of the most significant.

He uses behavioral data when testing new management solutions. In fact, when he hears that a company has decided to invest millions of dollars in initiatives like new workspace solutions or collaborative technology without testing them first, it frustrates him.

He finds it maddening that leaders forget to consider context when making decisions that impact how people work.

For example, he urges leaders to embrace the fact that just because a workspace solution works at another company doesn't mean it will for yours. This is simply because your people are not the same and the work they do is not the same. He implores leaders to use their own people data to evaluate

---

124 Ibid.

potential solutions so they can better understand how their people work.

One way to do this is with A/B testing. A/B testing is when you conduct an experiment where two or more solutions are tried out. The results are then analyzed to determine if the management solution solved the problem. According to Waber, some companies use *people analytics teams* and their job is to use behavioral data to A/B test recommended management solutions.[125]

BETTER BANK BRANCHES
In the case of the banks and their branch network, the objective was to get the lower-performing banks to improve their loan sales. After analyzing the data and the field trips, Waber and the team conducted one A/B test to measure management practice changes.

They had half of the lower-performing branches (group two) make changes to mirror what the high-performing branches (group one) did. In some cases, they got rid of their two floor locations. In others, they had people rotate and switch floors every couple months. In both cases the bank saw the loan sales go up by eleven percent in those branches, relative to the underperforming branches that did not implement the solutions.[126]

---

125 "Waber — Humanyze — TPH D2 Upheaval Energy Disruption Conference."
126 Ibid.

And regarding those banks with the outliers, the managers of new employees in these locations arranged for others in the bank to take the new employee out to lunch periodically in order to facilitate their integration into the branch. The bank covered the cost of lunch outings, which I'm guessing incentivized lunch hosts and made the conversations even more jovial.

Leaders,

Management solutions should be tested prior to rollout to ensure they work. They impact people. You wouldn't introduce massive software changes that impact large numbers of employees without first testing the change (at least I hope not). That same smartness needs to be applied to management practice changes too.

When you test a management practice solution and have data that proves it worked, your employees will embrace the disruptive change more readily and the benefits will come faster. Use people data to measure the results of a test. Use those results as part of the story when the change is fully rolled-out.

When employees see from data that the hard work you are asking them to do makes sense, they will be more likely to support the change, which in turn means faster adoption and quicker realization of benefits.

CHAPTER 15

TARGET OUTREACH

> Amazon told me we bought it and sure enough it was on bookshelves! I must have put it there when I cleaned Daniels room
>
> Delivered

> Lol thanks

When my high school student realized he needed *A Tale of Two Cities* for his literature class, and that he needed it as soon as possible, he texted me the link to the right edition on Amazon. I clicked the link to order it from my phone.

Then, the most amazing thing happened.

Amazon instantly told me we already had it.

Turns out, I had ordered the same book two years earlier for his older brother. I am guessing some smart person figured out that customers might order something they already have, then later realize this and be disappointed. This automated way to check and alert me when this happened both delighted and amused this busy mother.

Automation like that serves customers. It identifies a group of people that potentially need some support and provides it. In this case, the support was a well-timed prompt.

A DATA ENGINEER, A DATA SCIENTIST, AND A BUSINESSPERSON

In addition to being able to imagine the type of experience I had, someone at Amazon designed it, tested it, and put it in place. These people are commonly called data scientists. I called them brilliant.

I learned from Donncha Carroll of Axiom Consulting Partners that there are the two types of data professionals who make the magic happen: data engineers and data scientists. Carroll explained that it's important to make the distinction between these roles.

He told me, "Data scientists are usually responsible for running the models that make the connection between features (the measures of behavior) and outcomes (the business impact). Data engineers are responsible for acquiring, transforming and manipulating the data to get it into a form that the data scientists can use for modeling. They get the data ready for processing, which is often eighty percent of the work. Those two skillsets rarely sit within the same person, as they are quite different."

Carroll emphasized that you also need someone who understands the business to direct their efforts "which could be either the data scientist or data engineer if they understand the business well enough, but often it's neither of them." He said you need someone who can develop the right set of questions to answer. They do this by putting forward the right set of hypotheses to explain how different factors influence results, to focus the work on what matters most.

When you have a digital experience that listens to the data you are providing, it can delight or at least not annoy you. To make this possible you need experts who can visualize current experiences and how to make them better.

AMAZON SOLUTION THAT TARGETS CUSTOMERS
In the case of *A Tale of Two Cities* my guess is the business problem surfaced that there were too many items being returned. When the scientists analyzed all the return data and compared it to the order data, they must have seen that people were returning items they had ordered twice. When they saw this pattern, I picture them saying, "Voila!" Then the solution I experienced—the helpful prompt "you ordered this same item two years ago"—was imagined.

TARGETING UNIVERSITY'S MAJOR GIFT OFFICERS
Some organizations have data scientists analyze data for insights around where to focus teams with limited resources.

On the pristine twentieth floor of a South Michigan Avenue office building in Chicago, data scientists led by Dan Lowman at Grenzebach Glier and Associates help non-profit organizations determine the focus of their donor outreach.

To keep operating, many non-profits depend on supporter donations. Using data analysis to steer their efforts has proven valuable. A non-profit will often have one or more people responsible for outreach to donors. When a non-profit wants to make dramatic changes to elevate or expand their good work, they rely on donors to make what is called a "major" gift. When "major" gifts are being sought, the people working to find the right donors are called Major Gift Officers.

To help non-profits determine their outreach focus, Lowman and his team search for information about people—specific people. That is, people who have the means and passion to support the non-profit's mission. Lowman's team identifies these potential benefactors for non-profits' outreach strategies. They are matchmakers of sorts. They work to match a non-profit with people most likely to be passionate about their good work.

One of their clients, a large Ivy League university, called GG&A for help. They had hundreds of millions of data records about their 250,000 alumni. This information included things like years attended, courses taken, on-campus activities, and interactions with the school since leaving. The university needed help "mining the gold" from this information. They wanted to use the information to help establish outreach strategies for their Major Gift Officers.

Step 1: *Find the alumni who have the means and interest in giving to the university.*
Lowman and his team got to work looking at how their donors and prospective donors are "talking" to the University through their patterns of giving, event attendance,

volunteering, and all the other ways they choose to interact. This work got them part of the way to their answer. They knew which alumni would like to engage and give.

Next, Lowman's team got to work on determining ability to give. This was done using data external to the university, that is offered by companies like Claritas. This includes consumer behavioral information like shopping and technology preferences and online and offline media habits. When they mixed in this data, they were able to whittle their list of 250,000 alumni down to 13,000 graduates who had the ability to give a donation of $100,000 or more.

Step 2: Narrow down the list through interest and readiness to give to the university.
While it was great news that the university had such a large group of alumni with the potential to make large gifts, this group of 13,000 was still too large for their handful of Major Gifts Officers to manage. The officers' job is to establish relationships with prospects who have the capacity and affinity to donate a major monetary gift. It takes an individualized approach. This requires a lot of personal outreach over long periods of time. Thus, their potential donor list needed to be shorter and further refined by giving interest.

To accomplish this, Lowman's team designed and sent out an *interest and giving survey* to the list of 13,000 alumni. The survey responses resulted in a shorter list of 193 alumni. These alumni had identified themselves as *highly interested in the performing arts*, and as recent donors to *theaters*.

This specific finding was exactly what was needed for the university's small group of Major Gift Officers to build a *focused outreach strategy* they could execute.

Being able to use the University's alumni data, along with public data about spending habits, helped Lowman's team narrow the list. Their survey to that smaller alumni group gave them information that resulted in being able to provide the actionable list of potential donors to the Major Gifts Officers.

CHRO TARGETS EMPLOYEE WITH NEW WELLNESS POLICIES
"Deadman. That's what you'd be if it weren't for Karen."

It was a harsh, but accurate greeting that the young Chief Executive Officer received when he returned to work after a long, unplanned absence. While only in his early forties and seemingly healthy, the CEO had been living on borrowed time—only he didn't know it. His Chief Human Resources Officer (CHRO), Karen Mitrenga, had instituted a new wellness policy that resulted in him getting critical heart surgery after a routine wellness check that likely saved his life.[127]

In 2013, Moritz Erhardt was an intern working in London for the investment banking division at Bank of America. When he didn't show up for work one day, his friends checked his dorm room and found him dead. He had worked seventy-two hours straight, three nights in row.

---

[127] Story is a combination of narratives provided by Karen Mitrenga. Details modified to protect privacy.

At this time, investment banking interns prided themselves in having brutal hours, and often treated working through the night as a rite of passage.[128]

While Erhardt's death was found to be an epileptic seizure, it's noted that this fit could have been triggered by his long working hours.[129]

After this tragedy, Goldman Sachs was the first to modify their policies to change the intern experience. Bank of America and others followed suit.

They modified working hours and included various wellness programs for the interns, including programs where leaders expressed the need to address social-emotional wellbeing to interns.

Shortly after the tragedy, Lloyd Blankfein, then CEO of Goldman Sachs, told his interns that they shouldn't give over their whole lives to the firm. "You have to be interesting; you have to have interests away from the narrow thing of what you do," he said. "You have to be somebody who somebody else wants to talk to."[130]

Others beyond banking also heard the call to assess employee wellbeing in high-stress jobs, including Mitrenga's company. Her firm also decided to look at the health of their employees. They learned that the high stress work of their analysts

---

128 Day. "Moritz Erhardt: The Tragic Death Of A City Intern."
129 Neate. "Goldman Sachs Restricts Intern Workday To 17 Hours In Wake Of Burnout Death."
130 Ibid.

and others often resulted in poor lifestyle choices. Mitrenga knew something had to be done. She worked with a team and devised a Wellness Policy and supporting program that included requiring all employees over the age of forty to get an annual physical.

When the company's CEO was showing up on Mitrenga's list of those tardy with their annual physical, Mitrenga persistently hounded him until it was scheduled. Her hounding was a life saver. The CEO, who appeared healthy, learned about a critical heart condition at his annual physical, that resulted in him getting critical heart surgery.

Having the ability to track if targeted groups of employees at her company had completed their physical allowed Mitrenga to remind her CEO to get his physical. Mitrenga's Wellness Policy has remained place. It continues to target those whose work demands make them more vulnerable to unhealthy behaviors.

MS HEAD ENGINEER TARGETS TEAM MEMBER BEHAVIORS
Office 365 is a suite of software products developed by Microsoft Corporation that includes Microsoft Word, Excel, PowerPoint and Outlook. Each program serves a different purpose and is compatible with other programs included in the suite. Office is the most common form of software used in the Western world.[131]

---

131 Blaisdel, "*Office 365 – The Most Popular Cloud App In 2015 - Rick's Cloud.*"

Office 365 has a feature called MyAnalytics. MyAnalytics provide a dashboard that uses a person's data to show things. For example, an employee can see the breakdown of their "focus time" versus "collaboration" time. This means how often they were in meetings versus when they were not in meetings and available to "focus." They can also see how much time they spend working during typical office hours, compared to others in their company. They can see the breakdown of what they are doing during the time outside of their typical hours. For example were they in meetings, responding to emails, or doing focus work.[132]

I can't help wondering: What if Bank of America had a tool in place like Microsoft's MyAnalytics when Erhardt worked there? Could alarms have sounded warning Erhardt that his behavior was dangerous? Could others at Bank of America have been alerted to the pocket of employees enduring excessive, unhealthy stress? I don't know—maybe.

I know it is naïve to think a tool alone can save a life.

What I envision is bigger. It's a leader saying, "The wellbeing of our employees is important, and we are encouraging everyone to take care of themselves—here is a tool that can help you do that."

An executive at Workplace Analytics and MyAnalytics at Microsoft told me that by "putting people analytics data into the hands of individuals, individuals can start to make changes to make their lives better. MyAnalytics does this in

---

132 "Myanalytics Introduction - Workplace Intelligence."

a way that makes it as easy as possible to go from the data or the insight into a desired behavioral change."

MyAnalytics has a Wellbeing page that shows how well you are disconnecting from work during your time off, and suggests ways to reduce stress and burnout. While I know a web screen can't save a life, I like the idea that a company would embrace a tool like MyAnalytics to communicate that employee wellbeing is important. I like that my behavioral data can get into my hands and show me what's going on—then offer me some suggestions.

This executive explained to me that the behavior data of individuals can be looked at as a set to solve business problems. She provided me an example from her own company, Microsoft.

Too Many Meetings?

There was a group of engineers that felt they were in too many meetings. They didn't have enough time to do the coding necessary for their jobs. They felt like meetings were impacting their productivity, their work-life balance, and their happiness at work. There was a belief by some of their managers that this situation was the nature of their work and could not be helped.

Data analyzed

An analysis team at Microsoft was tasked to learn more. They aggregated the team's behavioral operations data, analyzed it, and learned some interesting things.

Fragmented day

They learned when looking at the meeting data that the Microsoft engineers were not having any more meetings than other similar groups of engineers in other companies. However, the way their meetings were scheduled was highly fragmented.

Someone would go to a meeting for an hour, have an hour free, then go to another meeting for an hour and have an hour free before another meeting. As a result, this engineer would not have large chunks of time where he or she could get into the focused flow state needed for coding work.

Bad habits revealed

Additionally, the analysis team found the employees that reported low work-life balance and associated dissatisfaction, had managers with bad habits. This group of managers' data showed that they "scheduled meetings after hours, sent emails on the weekends and after hours, replied all to everything, and/or had really large unstructured meetings."

Target identified

The analysis team met the MS Head engineer and shared the results of the analysis. He was relieved to learn that the nature of their work (engineering work) was not the problem rather it was the fragmented day and bad habits of some managers, including himself.

He knew these problems could be solved by him and his management team. He put together a workshop with his management team to come up with a meeting time policy. They established timeframes when meetings were targeted to occur, and when they would be off limits with minimal exceptions. This would increase the number of big blocks of time for engineers to delve deep into their work.

He also shared with management that he had seen the data demonstrating that he and some others needed to change some of their meeting and email behaviors to improve the experience of employees. He let them know he was committed to doing that and would reach-out to the others who also needed to work on their behaviors.

Leaders,

By analyzing data, you can see who needs to be targeted—be it with solutions or with the dedication of scarce resources.

- *Amazon targeted customers like me—people who were ordering items they didn't really need, and implemented a solution that prompted me with a smart question: "Are you sure you want to buy a book you already have?"*
- *Lowman's team found the donors for the small group of the University's Major Gift Officers to target—those most likely to have the passion and ability to support the University's strategic investment.*
- *The CHRO, Mitrenga, targeted her team members that were most likely to have wellbeing issues with both her company's new wellbeing policies and her policy adherence monitoring.*
- *The MS Head engineer targeted team members (including himself) with a strong message about which behavior*

changes needed to change in order to address team stress. Additionally, the data analysis demonstrated the need for a new meeting policy, one that I am guessing he challenged his target group to adopt sooner rather than later.

Aggregate your people data to find the targeted solutions and/or on which priority your resources should be focused. Mine the intelligence in your people data to gain organizational insights that allow you to focus your efforts in order to realize the largest impact possible.

CHAPTER 16
IGNITE GOAL SETTING. MONITOR PROGRESS

About two months after our son Chris was born, I remember seeing a pair of pants on our bed and wondering whose they were. I saw they were larger, so I thought they belonged to my husband but then they seemed even too big to be his. As I looked closer, I saw they were women's jeans. Then to my horror I realized they were mine. It was true, I had gained considerable weight when I was pregnant and was still much larger at that time than I thought I was.

As I shared the story later that day with my neighbor Jenny who also had a newborn, we had a good laugh. Then we talked about when and how I would get back to taking care of myself. Jenny had some good advice for me, as she always did.

It's hard to be self-aware sometimes. Especially without evidence, you can walk around thinking you are the picture of perfect physical health when in truth you are not. The hard data—like weight, heart rate, and cholesterol levels—let us know when we have some work to do to get physically healthy.

FACTS IGNITE ACTION

There's ample evidence that demonstrates when an individual needs to make a behavioral change having facts that demonstrate that change is needed work better than platitudes alone.

The popularity and success of Fitbit, investment apps, and iOS 12 Screen Time demonstrate that seeing your current state of affairs and being able to see progress is motivating.[133]

In the workplace, some employees are provided performance feedback quickly which in turn motivates them to improve. Many are not. They are left to assess for themselves how they are doing, in-between formal performance reviews.

IGEN'ERS AND GOAL SETTING

iGen'ers crave data. They consume data all day long in their personal lives. In doing this, they integrate different information, gain insights, and come to their own conclusions.

Ask an iGen'er about anything, and they will share what they know from the content they have already consumed. Plus if

---

[133] "Ios Introduces 12 New Features To Reduce Interruptions And Manage Screen Time,"

asked, they will dig into your question further, do research, and provide you insights—and do so quickly.

Some companies are integrating people data and using it to get **organizational insights** to address company challenges as shared in the proceeding chapters.

My research did not yield any examples of organizations integrating people data and providing employees their unique information so they each could get **individual insights** to address their personal challenges.

Should you provide an iGen'er their integrated people data along with what the company needs from the them (i.e. skills to develop, experience to have, counsel to seek), iGen'ers will see where they have gaps and set their goals.

MONITOR PROGRESS

Having data appeals to iGen'ers. They are avid consumers of online media and have spent a considerable amount of time online. For them, online is a place they are often present. Online is where employers should communicate the job challenges and growth opportunities for iGens. If the information is presented in a way where an iGen'er can select meaningful goals and easily monitor their progress, like the dashboard described in Chapter 1, it will be as popular and successful with iGen'ers as the Fitbit, brokerage apps, and the iOS 12 screen time tool have been with others.

Jon Briscoe, a professor at Northern Illinois University, contends that feelings of success in the workplace occur when people see that they can grow and meet job challenges by pursuing and attaining goals that are important and meaningful.

Having data that shows you the progress you have made, relative to where you were, reminds you of the control you have and encourages you to keep moving toward your goal.

Leaders,

iGen will be twenty percent of the workforce in 2020.[134] *Use your people data to ignite in your youngest workers the desire to set personal goals to both address their skill gaps and improve their wellbeing.*

Integrate your people data and provide each individual their data. Your iGen'ers will understand it. Use AI to complement their workplace digital experiences by setting up personalized prompts suggesting actions to take (e.g. skills to improve, experience to gain, counsel to seek from a manager or mentor), and applauding actions taken. [135] *Be sure to include a way to monitor progress—and, of course, make sure the integrated data is accessible on a smartphone or even a wristband.*

Organizations that inspire their iGen'ers to set and achieve goals related to wellbeing and new technology will find themselves with a connected workforce that's engaged, appreciative of the steady work, and eager to contribute to solving big problems.

---

134 Megan Dutta "Gen Z Is Coming To The Workforce—Are You Ready?"
135 AI stands for artificial intelligence

Organizations that don't demonstrate an understanding of iGens' need for data-driven career direction will have a hard time retaining them.[136]

Plus organizations should take note: with data privacy and security laws already here and with more on their way, soon any employee will be able to port their data from their employers.[137] [138] *Since iGen'ers crave data—and frankly have fun with it—many will ask for it, explore it on their own, and stay disconnected from their workplace.*

FITBIT MONITORING[139]

Barry Parkes knew that a lifestyle change was needed.

"I stepped on the scale in the workout room and it was 325. I was like—what? How did I get here? This is way higher than I ever thought I would be," says Parkes, who decided to commit to losing weight at that moment.

Parkes, an assistant principal at Rigby High School in Idaho, had been overweight and out of shape for twenty years. He didn't exercise and his eating habits were

---

136 Twenge, "Meet iGen: The New Generation Of Workers That Is Almost Everything Millennials Aren't."
137 The General Data Protection is in place.
138 The California Consumer Privacy Act is in place, but businesses will not need to honor requests for personal information access until January 2021. Anna Amodaj, Jennifer Daniels, Kathy Herman, David Oberly, Ana Tagvoryan. "Despite The Passage Of CCPA Employee Amendment, Employers Still Face Significant Compliance Burdens Under California's New Privacy Law." JD Supra. September 25, 2019.
139 Hepworth, "Assistant Principal Loses 110 Pounds, His Wife Loses 40, In Fitbit Transformation."

poor.

He's a math guy so he thought having a way to track would help. He asked his co-worker about Fitbit. She downloaded it on his phone. He went home that day, and since then he has kept track of every single thing he eats.

Using the Fitbit, he lost 110 pounds.

"I'm by no means an expert—which is an indication that anybody can do this," Parkes says. "It's not that hard if you just really want to do it. I think that commitment is the key."

Another key for Parks was having a simple way to track his progress.

BROKERAGE APP

Using a brokerage app as part of his strategy, Grant Sabatier was able to watch his money grow and he became a millionaire before age thirty.

"It took me exactly five years, three months, and six days to go from $2.26 in my bank account to $1.25 million and financial independence at the age of thirty. On that day, I've never taken a deeper breath," he says.[140]

Sabatier was unemployed, broke, and living with his

---

140 Sabatier, "My Story: $2.26 To Millionaire In 5 Years."

parents. One afternoon, he was hungry for a burrito. The twenty-something checked his account balance and learned that he had $2.26 in the bank. This low point was his wake-up call. Sabatier took an image of this balance and set a goal of saving so much money that he could retire early if he wanted. "I remember having this intense feeling of honestly just...lack of control," he says.

Sabatier found a job at a marketing agency. He took on side gigs to make extra cash. He studied more than 300 personal finance books and came up with his own strategies. They included deciding to make saving a daily habit, always looking for ways to keep expenses low, and daily monitoring of his funds.

Sabatier decided to invest at least five dollars a day. Each day he invested this extra money. He watched his funds grow and surpass a million dollars, keeping watch on his brokerage app. [141]

IOS 12 SCREEN TIME

Apple now has tools built into their iOS 12 (operating system) to help their customers understand and monitor the time they spend interacting with devices. The tools include Activity Reports and Screen Time.[142]

---

141 Marte. "This Chicago man saved $1 million by the time he was 30. Here's how he did it."
142 "iOS 12 Introduces New Features To Reduce Interruptions And Manage Screen Time.".

When my son Chris was home after his first semester of college, we found ourselves discussing the iPhone screen time tools. It was around seven in the evening. It was his third day home after his final exams, and he had been relaxing.

We compared our screen time metrics for something called "pickups" which is how often you "pick up" your phone throughout the day.

- My first pickup was at five a.m. It said since then I had picked up my phone fifty-one times.
- Chris's first pickup was nine a.m. It said he had subsequently picked up his phone a hundred and two times.

Then we compared our overall screen time data.

- My screen time was showing as one hour fifty-eight minutes.
- Chris's screen time was six hours thirty-nine minutes.

Then we looked at the breakdown of our screen time.

- For me, forty-eight minutes of my screen time was mostly attributed to a category called "productivity" (for me this was email), and the rest was mostly the social networking category (for me this mostly was my texting app).
- For Chris, six hours and fifteen minutes of his screen time was social networking (for him this was Snapchat, Twitter, Instagram) and the rest was mostly productivity (email).

When we discussed our screen time, I told Chris about Cal Newton, the computer science professor with the

"Digital Minimalism" philosophy that says we should be more intentional about how we use technology, and more aware of how technology uses us.[143]

A little over a month after this conversation, Chris's brother Daniel tipped me off that Chris had deleted a bunch of apps. This prompted me to reach out to him for a conversation about screen time.

I asked him if he had indeed deleted some apps. He said he had. He deleted Instagram, Facebook, TikTok, and Twitter. He had kept Snapchat and added the *Wall Street Journal* app. He explained his time on Snapchat was for periods of time that were ten or so minutes when he was directly engaging with friends.

His average screen time for the last week was around three and a half hours a day. I asked him how he was finding the change. He answered sincerely: "I like it. I'm not on my phone as much."

SOCIAL-EMOTIONAL SKILLS

Underdeveloped social-emotional skills sometimes happen when someone has not spent enough time in the "real world" integrating socially. Social-emotional skills can be strengthened.

Dr. James Mazza co-authored a curriculum called *DBT Skills in Schools: Skills Training for Emotional Problem*

---

143 Newport. "Avoiding Digital Distraction."

Solving for Adolescents. The DBT classes provide students a way to identify which skills need work, then track their progress.

DBT stands for dialectical behavior therapy. It is a type of therapy that's used to treat people struggling with strong emotional pain or what is called "dysregulation."

The skills included are: mindfulness, distress tolerance, emotion regulation, and interpersonal effectiveness. The DBT course is designed for everyone, not just those struggling (e.g. with anxiety or depression).[144]

One of the tools included in the class is a diary card. Dr. Mazza explains, "We know through research that knowledge gained does not equal behavior change." We needed a way to do behavioral data collection in the classroom to examine the adoption of the new skills and measure their effectiveness. Students track their use of the skills daily, then provide a qualitative rating if it was effective or not.

Additionally each week, students meet for ten minutes in pairs to talk about the skills they practiced last week. "How did it go? What got in the way? What was successful? If something got it the way, what is a way to overcome that?" Though it is important to note that if an adolescent does not feel comfortable sharing their situation, nor having their partner share, that certainly is an option and it's ok.

---

144 dbtinschools.com, accessed January 17, 2020.

The course was developed in 2006, before smartphones were in every student's hand. Dr. Mazza is now working on a diary card app that students can use on their phone to track skills learned in their classroom and their use of those skills during the week. Dr. Mazza wants to have the app paired with the skills training. The app would prompt a student who reports feeling frustration with "What do you need from your distress tolerance skills? Or what do you need from your emotion regulation skills?' and link to related content. These will be skills that the student is familiar with because they have learned them in the class.

CONCLUSION

I set out to find out why so many young adults were lonely and what employers could do to help.

The research led me down a path that showed me features added to social media apps were causing many people to spend unhealthy amounts of time online. The voices of concern were not loud enough to stop the attempts to brain hack people, so the harm continued.

The research also led me down a path that caused me to reflect on how I, as a parent, had neglected to keep my own children safe. I let them have unsupervised access to the Internet, and all that came with it. Like many, I got caught up in the excitement of new smartphones, and I regret it.

I learned that many young adults are lonely because as teens, they did not spend enough time in the real world developing the skills needed to have meaningful relationships with people—the type of relationships that encourage you and help you through setbacks. While online as teens, many were exposed to harsh toxic content and either experienced significant amounts of cyberbullying personally and/or witnessed it, unable to do much about it.

When it comes to the workplace, young adults can find both community and connection. What it will take is for leaders to acknowledge that technology has not just changed business processes and jobs, but also has fundamentally changed younger workers. They engage and work differently. Because of this, the workplace needs to adapt. Younger workers are most comfortable online, and that's where they will quickly get work done.

They consume data to gain insights in their personal lives and are eager to do the same at work. Organize your people data and provide it to these workers in a smart way that shows them which skills they need to develop and how to go about it—then watch it happen fast.

Equip your managers with the education and tools they need to manage people online and offline, and create community and connection for their employees. Plus, provide them education on how to work with data and use it to communicate, especially with younger workers.

Understand that the employee digital experience needs just as much (maybe more) attention and care as the lobbies, elevators, break-rooms, and workspaces where employees are. Integrate people data and use it to gain insights for how to make the employee digital experience more attractive and be smarter.

While it is true many young adults are lonely, employers can provide them realness, meaning, and belonging at work. Done right, they will find the hardest working group of employees to enter the workplace in a long time.

EPILOGUE

BEYOND YOUR COMPANY—CAN YOU BE THE BULLDOG LEADER SOCIETY NEEDS?

While there are some loud voices of concern about the mental health crisis—created in part by technology—they are not being heard.

As an expert in change management, it's clear to me what is missing: **a bulldog leader.**

In doing the research for this book, I learned the history around James Couzens. To me, he seems like the type of leader we could use now.

Couzens was a former executive of Ford Motor Company. He resigned in 1913 with stock worth $38 million, became

Detroit's commissioner of street railways, and later its police commissioner, mayor and, eventually, U.S. senator. He is described as looking and acting like a bulldog.

He took on the public and industry and shouldered extreme criticism to better society. I admire his choice to do hard social work versus quietly retiring.

From 1909 to 1916, cars exploded onto the scene in the United States. In seven years motorized vehicles in the States went from 200,000 to 2.25 million. It created chaos in urban neighborhoods. In 1917, Detroit and its suburbs, where Couzens lived, had 65,000 cars on the road. That same year there were 7,171 accidents with 168 deaths, and hundreds more injured.[145]

NO ONE ANTICIPATED THE DISRUPTION THE INTRODUCTION OF THE AUTOMOBILE WOULD HAVE ON DAILY LIFE.

Before cars, streets were a safe place for children to play and city dwellers to take a stroll. While there was an occasional streetcar or horse on the road, they could be anticipated well in advance and avoided. With cars, there was no warning. Daily, they were racing around corners and running over children playing on the streets. Cars brought mobility, but also death and destruction to urban neighborhoods.[146]

---

145 "1900-1930: The years of driving dangerously."
146 Ibid.

COUZENS TOOK THIS ON. HE RESTORED SAFETY.
Couzens put the needed order into Detroit—like pedestrian cross walks, stop signs, and no-parking zones. He called out related behavior changes needed, such as adhering to stop signs. He handled noisy objections to the newly imposed rules. He created consequences for offenders. When illegal parking continued to be a problem, he wrote in a 1917 annual police report that, "Educational methods did not bring about the desired results, so it was deemed advisable to institute a system of intensive disciplinary training." He started having offending cars towed. Within six months, the new Detroit Towing Squad hauled 10,737 cars. The transformational work that Couzens led eventually became a global model.[147]

WE NEED SAFETY RESTORED.
There are parallels between the disruption the automobiles caused then and the disruption the digital revolution is causing now.

We need a bulldog leader who:

- Understands that this mental health crisis was created by both brilliance and greed.
- Can push the ball of sedentary inertia over the hill to create action needed.
- Can pull our eyes off our screens long enough to understand the gravity of our unhealthy lifestyles.

---

147 Ibid.

- Has the social capital to influence technology and government leaders around the world to be accountable for doing the hard work of addressing this societal crisis.
- Has the fortitude to take the heat that will come from pushing to enact dramatic social change.
- Can create order from the chaos of the digital revolution.

Can you be the bulldog leader society needs?

ACKNOWLEDGEMENTS

Thank you to my husband John. Your support of me is always present. Thank you to my son Chris, for discussing the book with me, suggesting people I should interview, and letting me observe his screen time. Thank you to my son Daniel, "the iGen from the Midwest," for agreeing to attend Professor Eric Koester's lecture with me during family weekend at Georgetown—that moment in time is what sent me down this path (and we must admit, Prof. Koester's lecture had to be better than the Magic Show). Thank you to Prof. Koester, for answering my LinkedIn message after that lecture. As I told you when we first chatted, the skills you require your students to develop in order a write a non-fiction book will serve them well, not only in their careers but in their personal lives. You are showing them how to reach-out and connect with people. I applaud you. Thank you for letting me be part of your class of "professionals" turned creators. I've enjoyed the ride—especially being able to meet and be inspired by fellow authors who are incredible people I would have never met.

Thank you to brilliant researchers (Cal Newport, Susan Pinker, Jean Twenge, Daniel Coyle, Ben Sasse and others) who shared their wisdom in relatable books, whose pages I have read and reread as I connected your messages and wrestled with how leaders in the workplace can address the collisions occurring between the wellbeing of young adults and well-intentioned technology developers. Thank you to dozens of experts who granted my request for a personal interview, then shared their wisdom and point of view with me. I look forward to continuing our conversations.

Thank you to the numerous people I have worked with over the years, especially the managers I had as a young adult, Gerald Sparkman, Vijay Rangineni, Oscar Foster, Chuck Shoemaker, Scott Bates, and Bob Greco. We spend much of our lives "at work" and those experiences affect us and shape us. Many of those experiences have influenced this book—and for them I'm grateful. Thank you to my "networking" friends who appreciate the importance of pushing both each other and ourselves to get uncomfortable in order to grow. Thank you to Anita Jenke and the Career Transitions Center. I appreciate you letting me be a small part of the great work you do. Thank you to my parents and all the members of my extended family for the enthusiastic encouragement. Thank you to my friends, my St. Andrew community, my St. Ignatius community, those from the hometown of my youth—Appleton, Wisconsin—and those I met when I was a young adult at Marquette University, Loyola University of Chicago, and the Jesuit Volunteer Corp. God has blessed me with solid relationships. I wish the same for every young adult I encounter.

Thank you to my editors, Elissa Graeser, Bailee Noella, Michelle Felich and Gina Champagne, your encouragement at critical moments has been a game-changer. Thank you to Grzegorz Laszczyk for back and forth on interior design and to Nikola Tikoski and Gjorgji Pejkovski for patiently shepparding me through the cover design process. Thank you everyone at Creator Institute and New Degree Press (especially Brian Bies—do you ever sleep?). Thank you to my helpful Beta Readers especially my sister and shadow editor, Eileen Speidel, my mother, Mary Louise Hildebrandt, my son, Daniel McFarland, my niece, Annie Longfellow and my dear friend, Happy Peris.

And thank you to everyone who pre-ordered the eBook, paperback—single and multiple copies—and helped spread the word about this book, especially my brother Kevin Long who was the first to pre-order (after Prof. Koester).

I am sincerely grateful to each one of you:

Alyson Nash, Angela Allen, Annabelle Clinger, Ann Freeman, Anne M Weiland, Anonymous, Anthony Sarnowski, April Lara, Ashley Ford, Barbara Hoban, Barbara Macintyre, Brian Long, Bridget Doyle-Olson, Cara J Lindell, Cate Kinder, Catherine Madden, Cecilia Loftus, Cheryl Murphy, Christa Arite, Colleen Brennan, Colleen Campbell, Darci Forrest, Denise Olsen, Dennis Vanooyen, Donald E. Roberts, Donna Venteicher, Eileen Herber, Eileen Neville, Eileen Sethna, Eileen Speidel, Elizabeth and Dave Tesch, Emily Early Kehrberg, Eric Koester, Frances Butler, H. Richard Collins Jr, Happy Peris, Heather Way Kitzes, James R Long, Jessica Worny Janicki, Jim McFarland, John and Julie Lucas, John and Sandra McFarland, John V. and Patricia Lucas Jr, Julie Nelson, Kathleen Long O.P., Kathleen Murdock, Kathy Scherer, Katie Guzzardo, Kelly Johnson, Kelly Rice, Kerry Rebora, Kevin and Margaret Long, Kevin M Collins, Kevin Ryan, Kim A Nugent, Kimberly Lord Arndt, Laura Biskupic, Leeann Enright, Lisbeth Blankenship, Lorene Meyer, Lori

Igleski, Lori Lazzara, Lynn A Walker, Lynn Deely, Madeleine Ruff, Marcia Bremner, Maribeth Lynch, Marisa Wills, Mary Ann McCully, Mary Beth and Tony LoVerdi, Mary Beth Sheehan, Mary Kay Pond, Mary Langhenry, Mary Louise Hildebrandt, Mary Patronik, Mary Rose Armstrong, Mary Sue Gurka, Megan and Scott Leadbetter, Melissa Rotunno, Michael and Jennifer Lucas, Michele Helffrich, Michelle Roberts, Molly Cullen House, Pamela Madura, Patricia B. Cook, Patricia Brady, Patrick B. Long, Peggy Lord, Ramien Rosillo, Renee M. Dalton, Rita Long, Robert Greco, Robert Ruff, Rose Arendarczyk, Scott Hinton, Sevgi Dasdelen, Sheila Long, Sheryl Markov, Stephanie Arcuri, Susanne Collins, Suzanne Voss, Thomas A. Kelly, Thomas Bauer, Thomas E. Geerdts, Tina Bowness, Timothy Long, Tom and Kathy Long, Tom Hildebrandt, Tom Long, Tom and Colleen Traxler, Tricia Luzadder, Vijay Rangineni, William and Joanne Suneson

APPENDIX

INTRODUCTION

Abbott, Brianna. "Youth Suicide Rate Increased 56% In Decade, CDC Says." *Wall Street Journal,* October 17, 2019. https://www.wsj.com/articles/youth-suicide-rate-rises-56-in-decade-cdc-says-11571284861.

Allen, Mike. "Sean Parker Unloads On Facebook: "God Only Knows What It's Doing To Our Children's Brains." November 9, 2017, *Axios.* https://www.axios.com/sean-parker-unloads-on-facebook-god-only-knows-what-its-doing-to-our-childrens-brains-1513306792-f855e7b4-4e99-4d60-8d51-2775559c2671.html.

Balakrishnan, Anita. "Facebook Should Be Regulated Like A Cigarette Company, Says Salesforce CEO". January 23, 2018, CNBC. *https://www.cnbc.com/2018/01/23/salesforce-ceo-marc-benioff-says-regulate-facebook-like-tobacco.html.*

"Being Watched At Work: Workplace Surveillance Perceptions" Guide, Studies, Simplyhired.com. Accessed on January 23, 2020. https://www.simplyhired.com/guide/studies/being-watched-at-work.

"iGen Quotes By Jean M. Twenge." Accessed January 18, 2020. *Goodreads.Com.* https://www.goodreads.com/work/

quotes/53990370-igen-why-today-s-super-connected-kids-are-growing-up-less-rebellious-m.

McKinsey Global Institute, "Jobs Lost, Jobs Gained: Workforce Transitions in a Time of Automation," December 2017, *Mckinsey.Com*. https://www.mckinsey.com/~/media/mckinsey/featured insights/Future of Organizations/What the future of work will mean for jobs skills and wages/MGI-Jobs-Lost-Jobs-Gained-Report-December-6-2017.ashx.

"New Cigna Study Reveals Loneliness at Epidemic Levels in America," Newsroom, news releases, *Cigna, A Global Health Insurance And Health Service Company*. 2020. https://www.cigna.com/newsroom/news-releases/2018/new-cigna-study-reveals-loneliness-at-epidemic-levels-in-america.

Newport, Cal. "Avoiding Digital Distraction" August 9, 2019, produced by Innovation Hub, podcast, 30 minutes. https://podcasts.google.com/?feed=aHRocHM6Ly9mZWVkcy53Z-2JoLm9yZy8xMDYvZmVlZC1yc3MueG1s&episode=cHJ4X-zEwNl9kZjM3OTY3Mi1mNzAzLTQyYTgtYmQ2ZC05M-zYoMGVmNjRmNmI&hl=en&ved=2ahUKEwi9yqmtpZb-nAhWIQcoKHbgqBCUQjrkEegQIARAE&ep=6.

Sasse, Ben. *Them: Why We Hate Each Other And How To Heal*. St. Martin's Press, 2018. 1-15. 48-49, 55-62

Shahi, Rohin. The Z Factor: How to Lead Gen Z to Workplace Success. New Degree Press, 2019. 35. 41-42, 45, 58.

Skeldon, Paul. "69% Of Consumers Want An Individualised Customer Experience Yet Only 40% Of Brands Offer One" Internet Retailing. October 24, 2017 (September 1, 2019) https://internetretailing.net/mobile-theme/mobile-theme/69-of-consumers-want-an-individualised-customer-experience-yet-only-40-of-brands-offer-one-15777.

Twenge, Jean M. "iGen: The Smartphone Generation." March 9, 2018. *Tedx Talks*, Lagunablanca School, *Youtube*. https://www.youtube.com/watch?v=UA8kZZS_bzc.

Twenge, Jean. *"iGen: Why Today's Super-Connected Kids Are Growing Up Less Rebellious, More Tolerant, Less Happy—And Completely Unprepared For Adulthood (And What This Means For The Rest Of Us)*, Atria Books, 2017. 90-91, 312-313.

Twenge, Jean M. "Meet iGen: The New Generation Of Workers That Is Almost Everything Millennials Aren't". *Quartz At Work*, January 11, 2018, https://qz.com/work/1177712/igen-the-new-young-generation-of-workers-is-almost-everything-that-millennials-are-not/.

Twenge, Jean M. "Have Smartphones Destroyed A Generation?". *The Atlantic*. September 2017 Issue. https://www.theatlantic.com/magazine/archive/2017/09/has-the-smartphone-destroyed-a-generation/534198/.

Pinker, Susan. *The Village Effect: Why Face-To-Face Contact Matters*. Canada: Atlantic Books, 2014. 44-72.

Weller, Chris. "Silicon Valley Parents Are Raising Their Kids Tech-Free—And It Should Be A Red Flag". *Business Insider*. February 18, 2018. https://www.businessinsider.com/silicon-valley-parents-raising-their-kids-tech-free-red-flag-2018-2.

HOW TO READ THIS BOOK
N/A

CHAPTER 1: THE TIME IS NOW TO USE PEOPLE DATA
Cornerstoneondemand.Com. glossary, people-data, Accessed on January 25, 2020. https://www.cornerstoneondemand.com/glossary/people-data.

Holt-Lunstad, Julianne, Timothy B. Smith, and J. Bradley Layton. 2010. "Social Relationships And Mortality Risk: A Meta-Analytic Review." *Plos Medicine* 7 (7): e1000316. doi:10.1371/journal.pmed.1000316.

Pinker, Susan. "Transcript Of "The Secret To Living Longer May Be Your Social Life." TED2017. https://www.ted.com/talks/susan_pinker_the_secret_to_living_longer_may_be_your_social_life/transcript

Stone, Will. 2015. "Divorce? That's Not As Stressful As Moving Home". *Express.Co.Uk*. https://www.express.co.uk/news/uk/574171/Divorce-stressful-moving-home.

CHAPTER 2: RETOOL YOUR MANAGERS
Babington-Ashaye, Yemi. "What Do Young People Care About? We Asked 26,000 Of Them." World Economic Forum. November 8, 2016, https://www.weforum.org/agenda/2016/11/what-do-young-people-care-about-we-asked-26-000-of-them/.

Picchi, Aimee. "How Technology Can Lead To Loneliness In The Workplace." *Cbsnews.Com*. November 13, 2018, https://www.

cbsnews.com/news/how-technology-can-lead-to-loneliness-in-the-workplace/.

Pinker, Susan. *"The Village Effect: Why Face-To-Face Contact Matters"* Canada: Atlantic Books, 2014. 190-191 196-197, 209-211

Rapacon, Stacy. "The Skills Employers Are Looking For" *CNBC*.com December 2, 2015. https://www.cnbc.com/2015/12/01/the-skills-employers-are-looking-for.html.

"Social-Emotional Skills." 2020. Home, Toolkit, *Nationalmentoringresourcecenter.Org*. Accessed on January 24, 2020. https://nationalmentoringresourcecenter.org/index.php/toolkit/item/247-social-emotional-skills.html.

"The Heart Of What We Do" - Dr. Vivek Murthy On Rediscovering Meaning In Medicine". Newsroom, Blog, *ACGME*.org, March 21, 2019. https://acgme.org/Newsroom/Blog/Details/ArticleID/8071/The-Heart-of What-We-Do-Dr-Vivek-Murthy-on-Rediscovering-Meaning-in-Medicine.

Ticak, Mark "What Does Irl Mean?" 2016. Writing, Grammarly. Accessed on January 23, 2020. *https://www.grammarly.com/blog/irl-meaning/*.

Twenge, Jean. *iGen: Why Today's Super-Connected Kids Are Growing Up Less Rebellious, More Tolerant, Less Happy—And Completely Unprepared For Adulthood (And What This Means For The Rest Of Us)* Atria Books, 2017. 101-102,152-153, 19

Twenge, Jean M. "Meet iGen: The New Generation Of Workers That Is Almost Everything Millennials Aren't." Quartz At

Work, January 11, 2018, https://qz.com/work/1177712/igen-the-new-young-generation-of-workers-is-almost-everything-that-millennials-are-not/.

Vilhauer, Ph.D., Jennice. "This Is Why Ghosting Hurts So Much." 2020. *Psychology Today*. November 27, 2015. https://www.psychologytoday.com/us/blog/living-forward/201511/is-why-ghosting-hurts-so-much.

CHAPTER 3- BETTER EMPLOYEE EXPERIENCE

"Award Winning Employee Resource Groups." About Dell, Diversity & Inclusion, Employee Resource Groups. *Dell*.com. Accessed February 1, 2020, https://www.dell.com/learn/us/en/uscorp1/diversity-resource-groups.

Bailie, Ian. February 19, 2019. "How Can HR Tech Help Users to Own Their Data," My Future HR.com.

Dodd, Matthew. "Building Trust Through Pet Pics? Are You Barking Mad?!" *TECHCOMMUNITY.MICROSOFT.COM*. March 19, 2019 https://techcommunity.microsoft.com/t5/yammer-blog/building-trust-through-pet-pics-are-you-barking-mad/ba-p/353752.

"Where Do People You May Know Suggestions Come From On Facebook?" Friending, People You May Know, Facebook Help Centre, *Facebook.Com*. Accessed January 24, 2020, https://www.facebook.com/help/163810437015615?helpref=related.

CHAPTER 4 - DATA PRIVACY AND ETHICS

Amodaj, Anna, Jennifer Daniels, Kathy Herman, David Oberly, Ana Tagvoryan. "Despite The Passage Of CCPA Employee Amendment, Employers Still Face Significant Compliance Burdens Under California's New Privacy Law." JD Supra. September 25, 2019, https://www.jdsupra.com/legalnews/despite-the-passage-of-ccpa-employee-93890/.

"Being Watched At Work: Workplace Surveilance Perceptions" Guide, Studies, Simplyhired.com. Accessed on January 23, 2020. https://www.simplyhired.com/guide/studies/being-watched-at-work.

"Bill Text - AB-375 Privacy: Personal Information: Businesses.". Bill Information, California Legislative Information, Accessed January 24, 2020, *Leginfo.Legislature.Ca.Gov.* https://leginfo.legislature.ca.gov/faces/billTextClient.xhtml?bill_id=201720180AB375.

"Salesforce.com" home, company, ethical-and-human-sue, Accessed March 1, 2020, https://www.salesforce.com/company/ethical-and-humane-use/

"What Is GDPR, The EU'S New Data Protection Law?" GDPR.Eu. Accessed January 24, 2020, *GDPR.Eu.* https://gdpr.eu/what-is-gdpr/.

"What Are The GDPR Fines?" Accessed January 24, 2020, *GDPR. Eu.* https://gdpr.eu/fines/.

CHAPTER 5 - TYPES OF PEOPLE DATA
N/A

CHAPTER 6 - WELLBEING DATA

Aldana, Dr. Steve. 2020. "What Is Wellness? With No Wellness Program Definition It's Everything". blog, wellsteps.com, last updated January 17, 2020. https://www.wellsteps.com/blog/2020/01/02/what-is-wellness-program-definition/#What_is_Wellness_and_Why_Do_We_Need_a_Wellness_Program_Definition.

Denizet-Lewis, Benoit. "Why Are More American Teenagers Than Ever Suffering From Severe Anxiety?" *Nytimes.Com*. October 11, 2017, https://www.nytimes.com/2017/10/11/magazine/why-are-more-american-teenagers-than-ever-suffering-from-severe-anxiety.html.

"Employees Want To Take Control Of Their Wellbeing With Mobile Access To Services". October 3, 2018. US. blog, LifeWorks. https://www.lifeworks.com/blog/employees-want-to-take-control-of-their-wellbeing-with-mobile-access-to-services/.

Lui, Shanhoung. "Fitbit -Statistics & Facts." Technology & Telecommunications, Consumer Electronics, Statista.com, October 17, 2019 2020. *Www.Statista.Com*. https://www.statista.com/topics/2595/fitbit/.

Richardson, Jillian. "Opinion | What America's Loneliest Generation Suggests About Modern Interaction". January 1, 2019, *NBC News*, https://www.nbcnews.com/think/opinion/lonely-you-re-not-alone-america-s-young-people-are-ncna945446.

Twenge, Jean M. "Have Smartphones Destroyed A Generation?" *The Atlantic.* September 2017 Issue. https://www.theatlantic.com/magazine/archive/2017/09/has-the-smartphone-destroyed-a-generation/534198/.

Williams, LMFT, CEAP, Patrick. "Power To The People: The Changing Face of Employee Wellbeing". Feature. *Worldatwork. Org.* September 2019, https://www.worldatwork.org/workspan/articles/power-to-the-people?utm_source=Direct&utm_medium=eNewsletter&utm_term=workspan_weekly_ls_subscribe_wkspan_wkly_all&utm_content=Mixed&utm_campaign=ED_ANWLWKS1937.

CHAPTER 7- ENGAGEMENT DATA

"40% Of Young Adults Exhibit Perfectionist Tendencies – It's Not Good!" Carinasciences. October 6, 2019. *Carinasciences.Com.* https://carinasciences.com/2019/10/06/40-of-young-adults-exhibit-perfectionist-tendencies-its-not-good/."

Homeboy Industries.com." home, homeboyindustries.org, Accessed January 24, 2020, https://homeboyindustries.org/.

Bradt, George. "Be Like Zappos' Tony Hsieh - Answer Three Key Onboarding Due Diligence Questions," *August 10, 2011, Forbes. Com.* https://www.forbes.com/sites/georgebradt/2011/08/10/be-like-zappos-tony-hsieh-answer-three-key-onboarding-due-diligence-questions/#5df6a98db5bb.

Caine, Aine. "13 Signs You're In The Right Job, Even If It Doesn't Feel Like It." November 30, 2017. *The Independent.*co.uk https://

www.independent.co.uk/life-style/jobs-13-signs-right-role-work-employment-offices-companies-a8084686.html.

Croswell, Alexis. "20 Simple Employee Engagement Survey Questions You Should Ask." *Culture Amp Blog.* Accessed January 24, 2020, https://www.cultureamp.com/blog/employee-engagement-survey-questions/.

Coyle, Daniel. *The Culture Code.* Bantum Books, 2018. xv-xx.

"iGen Quotes By Jean M. Twenge." Accessed January 24, 2020. *Goodreads.Com.* https://www.goodreads.com/work/quotes/53990370-igen-why-today-s-super-connected-kids-are-growing-up-less-rebellious-m.

Kruse, Kevin. "What Is Employee Engagement," *Forbes.Com.* June 22, 2012, https://www.forbes.com/sites/kevinkruse/2012/06/22/employee-engagement-what-and-why/#6172bffb7f37.

Newport, Cal. *Avoiding Digital Distraction.* August 9, 2019, produced by Innovation Hub, podcast, 30 minutes. https://podcasts.google.com/?feed=aHR0cHM6Ly9mZWVkcy53Z-2JoLm9yZy8xMDYvZmVlZC1yc3MueG1s&episode=cHJ4X-zEwNl9kZjM3OTY3Mi1mNzAzLTQyYTgtYmQ2ZC05M-zYoMGVmNjRmNmI&hl=en&ved=2ahUKEwi9yqmtpZb-nAhWIQcoKHbgqBCUQjrkEegQIARAE&ep=6

O'Donnell, Jayne. "Teens Aren't Socializing in the Real World. And That's Making Them Super Lonely." March 20, 2019, *USAToday.com* https://www.usatoday.com/story/news/health/2019/03/20/teen-loneliness-social-media-cell-phones-suicide-isolation-gaming-cigna/3208845002/

Pinker, Susan. *The Village Effect: Why Face-To-Face Contact Matters*" Canada: Atlantic Books, 2014. 4. 90-91.

"Psychological Safety Defined." Friday.app Accessed February 6, 2020, https://www.friday.app/p/what-is-psychological-safety

Robins, Alison. "How To Properly Measure Employee Engagement."*Officevibe*. July 3, 2017, https://officevibe.com/blog/why-employee-engagement-is-hard-to-quantify.

Twenge, Jean M. "Have Smartphones Destroyed A Generation?". *The Atlantic*. September 2017 Issue. https://www.theatlantic.com/magazine/archive/2017/09/has-the-smartphone-destroyed-a-generation/534198/.

CHAPTER 8 - PERFORMANCE DATA

Newport, Cal. *Avoiding Digital Distraction*. August 9, 2019, produced by Innovation Hub, podcast, 30 minutes. https://podcasts.google.com/?feed=aHRocHM6Ly9mZWVkcy53Z-2JoLm9yZy8xMDYvZmVlZC1yc3MueG1s&episode=cHJ4X-zEwNl9kZjM3OTY3Mi1mNzAzLTQyYTgtYmQ2ZC05M-zYoMGVmNjRmNmI&hl=en&ved=2ahUKEwi9yqmtpZb-nAhWIQcoKHbgqBCUQjrkEegQIARAE&ep=6

Pinker, Susan. *The Village Effect: Why Face-To-Face Contact Matters*, Canada: Atlantic Books, 2014.

Robinson, Mike. "How Gambling Distorts Reality And Hooks Your Brain." *Fast Company*. August 14, 2018, https://www.fastcompany.com/90217918/how-gambling-distorts-reality-and-hooks-your-brain.

Ryan, Liz. "How To Manage Your Boss — Ten Dos And Don'ts." *Forbes.Com*. January 28, 2018, https://www.forbes.com/sites/lizryan/2018/01/28/how-to-manage-your-boss-ten-dos-and-donts/#3291200c3142.

Zenger, Jack and Joseph Folkman. "What Great Listeners Actually Do." *Harvard Business Review*. July 14, 2016, https://hbr.org/2016/07/what-great-listeners-actually-do.

CHAPTER 9 - PERSONAL DEVELOPMENT DATA

Doyle, PCC, CPC, ELI-MP, Heather. *Does Coaching Work? New Scientific Evidence Points to Yes*. blog, ipeccoaching.com Accessed January 24, 2020, https://www.ipeccoaching.com/blog/does-coaching-work-new-scientific-evidence-points-to-yes

Gerber, Scott. "11 Best Tools For Setting And Tracking Goals." *Business.Com*. January 13, 2015, https://www.business.com/articles/11-best-tools-for-setting-and-tracking-goals

Jenkins, Ryan. "This Is The No. 1 Thing Millennials Consider When Starting A Job." *Inc.Com*. January 16, 2018, https://www.inc.com/ryan-jenkins/want-to-retain-more-millennials-in-2018-offer-this-1-thing.html.

Newport, Cal. *Digital Mimimalism: Choosing A Focused Life In A Noisy World*. Penguin. 2019.6-20

Zimmerman, B. J., Bandura, A., & Martinez-Pons, M. (1992). Self-motivation for academic attainment: The role of self-efficacy beliefs and personal goal setting. *American Educational Research Journal, 29*(3), 663–676. https://doi.org/10.2307/1163261

CHAPTER 10 - OPERATIONS DATA

Augustinos, Theodore, Laura Ferguson, Ben FrazziniKendrick, Emily Holpert, Sean Kilian, Ricardo Lopez, Glenn Pudelka, Molly McGinnis Stine, Elizabeth Tosaris, Locke Lord LLP. Jdsupra.com, August 20, 2019, https://www.jdsupra.com/legal-news/ccpa-guide-does-personal-information-87475/

Get2whatmatters.Com. https://www.get2whatmatters.com/blog-1.

Sprangler, Nancy, PhD, OTR/L." Workplace Mental Health - Pacific Gas & Electric." case studies, *Workplacementalhealth. Org.* Accessed January 24, 2020, http://www.workplacementalhealth.org/Case-Studies/Pacific-Gas-Electric.

CHAPTER 11 - USING PEOPLE DATA

N/A

CHAPTER 12- DETECT PROBLEMS. PROMOTE SAFETY.

Elkin, Peter. "The Confessions of Andy Fastow." *Fortune.* July 1, 2013, https://fortune.com/2013/07/01/the-confessions-of-andy-fastow/.

Gupta, Shashank. "Sentiment Analysis: Concept, Analysis and Applications." Towardscience.com, January 7, 2018, https://towardsdatascience.com/sentiment-analysis-concept-analysis-and-applications-6c94d6f58c17

Rheem, Don. 2020. "William Kahn: Father Of Employee Engagement," *Donrheem.Com.* January 12, 2018, https://donrheem.com/william-kahn-father-of-employee-engagement/.

Waber, Ben. "Creating Better Organizations Based On How Its Members Interact," liftconference, *Youtube.* November 29, 2014, https://www.youtube.com/watch?v=PJC1h6p7CAU.

CHAPTER 13 - ANSWER QUESTIONS. REAFFIRM.

Bastone, Nick. "Salesforce's Chief People Officer Explains How And Why The Company Has Spent $8.7 Million To Close Its Gender Pay Gap." *Business Insider.* December 15, 2018, https://www.businessinsider.com/cindy-robbins-salesforce-equal-pay-2018-11.

Stahl, Leslie. "Leading By Example To Close The Gender Pay Gap." Video. *60 Minutes, Cbsnews.Com.* April 15, 2018, https://www.cbsnews.com/news/salesforce-ceo-marc-benioff-leading-by-example-to-close-the-gender-pay-gap/.

CHAPTER 14 - TEST SOLUTIONS. SOLVE PROBLEMS.

"Ben Waber — Humanyze — TPH D2 Upheaval Energy Disruption Conference." Tudor, Pickering, Holt & Co., Uploaded October 30, 2018. *Vimeo.* https://vimeo.com/297995676.

"Mapping Employee Chitchat Can Reveal Information Blockages." *Rework.Withgoogle.Com.* March 16, 2017, https://rework.withgoogle.com/blog/mapping-employee-interactions-reveals-networks/.

CHAPTER 15 - TARGET OUTREACH

Blaisdel, Rick. *"Office 365 – The Most Popular Cloud App In 2015 - Rick's Cloud."* Rick's Cloud. November 11, 2015, https://rickscloud.com/office-365-the-most-popular-cloud-app-in-2015/.

Day, Elizabeth. "Moritz Erhardt: The Tragic Death Of A City Intern." *The Guardian*. October 5, 2013, https://www.theguardian.com/business/2013/oct/05/moritz-erhardt-internship-banking.

"Myanalytics Introduction - Workplace Intelligence." *Docs.Microsoft.Com*. Accessed January 24, 2020. https://docs.microsoft.com/en-us/workplace-analytics/myanalytics/mya-landing-page.

Neate, Rupert. "Goldman Sachs Restricts Intern Workday To 17 Hours In Wake Of Burnout Death." *The Guardian*. June 17, 2015, https://www.theguardian.com/business/2015/jun/17/goldman-sachs-interns-work-hours.

CHAPTER 16 - IGNITE GOAL SETTING. MONITOR PROGRESS.

Amodaj, Anna, Jennifer Daniels, Kathy Herman, David Oberly, Ana Tagvoryan. "Despite The Passage Of CCPA Employee Amendment, Employers Still Face Significant Compliance Burdens Under California's New Privacy Law." JD Supra. September 25, 2019, https://www.jdsupra.com/legalnews/despite-the-passage-of-ccpa-employee-93890/.

Dbtinschools.com. Accessed January 24, 2020, http://www.dbtinschools.com/.

"DBT® Skills In Schools: Skills Training For Emotional Problem Solving For Adolescents – Behavioral Tech." 2020. *Behavioraltech.Org.* https://behavioraltech.org/store/books/dbt-skills-schools-skills-training-emotional-problem-solving-adolescents/.

Dutta, Megan. "Gen Z Is Coming To The Workforce—Are You Ready?" *ResidentialSystems.com.* July 15, 2019, https://www.residentialsystems.com/blogs/gen-z-is-coming-to-the-workforce-are-you-ready.

Hepworth, Natalia. "Assistant Principal Loses 110 Pounds, His Wife Loses 40, In Fitbit Transformation. *EastIdahoNews.com.* and Youtube. October 2, 2018, https://www.eastidahonews.com/2018/10/man-loses-110-pounds-his-wife-loses-40-in-fitbit-transformation/.*Youtube.* https://www.youtube.com/watch?v=2B02Zj5ez9g.

"Ios 12 Introduces New Features To Reduce Interruptions And Manage Screen Time." 2020. *Apple Newsroom.* Apple.com June 4, 2018, https://www.apple.com/newsroom/2018/06/ios-12-introduces-new-features-to-reduce-interruptions-and-manage-screen-time/.

Marte, Jonnelle. "This Chicago man saved $1 million by the time he was 30. Here's how he did it." March 29, 2017, *Chicagotribune.Com.* https://www.chicagotribune.com/business/success/ct-personal-finance-money-saving-tips-20170329-story.html.

Newport, Cal. *Avoiding Digital Distraction.* August 9, 2019, produced by Innovation Hub, podcast, 30 minutes. https://podcasts.google.com/?feed=aHR0cHM6Ly9mZWVkcy53Z-

2JoLm9yZy8xMDYvZmVlZC1yc3MueG1s&episode=cHJ4XzEwNl9kZjM3OTY3Mi1mNzAzLTQyYTgtYmQ2ZCo5MzYoMGVmNjRmNmI&hl=en&ved=2ahUKEwi9yqmtpZbnAhWIQcoKHbgqBCUQjrkEegQIARAE&ep=6.

Sabatier, Grant. "My Story: $2.26 To Millionaire In 5 Years." millennialmoney.com, December 18, 2019, https://millennialmoney.com/grant-sabatier/.

Twenge, Jean M. "Meet iGen: The New Generation Of Workers That Is Almost Everything Millennials Aren't". Quartz At Work, January 11, 2018, https://qz.com/work/1177712/igen-the-new-young-generation-of-workers-is-almost-everything-that-millennials-are-not/.

CLOSING

N/A

EPILOGUE

"1900-1930: The years of driving dangerously." Special to *The Detroit News*, *Detroitnews.Com*. April 26, 2015, https://www.detroitnews.com/story/news/local/michigan-history/2015/04/26/auto-traffic-history-detroit/26312107/.

www.ingramcontent.com/pod-product-compliance
Lightning Source LLC
LaVergne TN
LVHW011811060526
838200LV00053B/3739